W9-CTY-408

A GOOD MOM'S

Guide to Making

BAD

CHOICES

A GOOD MOM'S
Guide to Making BAD CHOICES

Jamilah Mapp and Erica Dickerson

HarperOne
An Imprint of HarperCollins*Publishers*

A GOOD MOM'S GUIDE TO MAKING BAD CHOICES. Copyright © 2023 by
Good Moms Bad Choices LLC. All rights reserved. Printed in the United
States of America. No part of this book may be used or reproduced in
any manner whatsoever without written permission except in the case of
brief quotations embodied in critical articles and reviews. For information,
address HarperCollins Publishers, 195 Broadway, New York, NY 10007.

HarperCollins books may be purchased for educational, business,
or sales promotional use. For information, please email the
Special Markets Department at SPsales@harpercollins.com.

FIRST EDITION

Illustrations © Shutterstock, Inc.

Library of Congress Cataloging-in-Publication
Data is available upon request.

ISBN 978-0-06-316197-9

23 24 25 26 27 LBC 5 4 3 2 1

This book has been both a manifestation of love and ceremony of release. We would like to dedicate this book to our daughters: may you always walk to the beat of your own drum. To our mothers, who birthed us to be trailblazers, and to all the women we've met on our voyage and all the women we will meet on this path: thank you for shaping us through conversation, lessons, and love.

Erica Milah

CONTENTS

INTRODUCTION

Two moms walk into a bar: one desperately seeking mommy friends, the other on the brink of a breakup, both with tequila in hand . . .

Cue "We Found Love" by Rihanna.

That's how we, Jamilah and Erica, met seven years ago as new moms finding our way. We jumped into motherhood from different places but with the same goal: get married, break generational curses, and live happily ever after. Of course, this being real life, things didn't quite turn out that way.

Warning: This is not your typical mommy how-to guide. In the pages that follow, you will hear both of our voices and the stories that led us to being good moms who embrace their bad choices. These choices and our friendship have been monumental to our growth and healing as women and evolution as modern-day mothers. Through sharing on our podcast radically honest stories about topics ranging from birth and sex to abuse and starting over, we have unlocked the cheat code to combating shame, guilt, and the toxic motherhood complex. But now, allow us to tell you how it all began.

MILAH

People call me Milah, but my government name is Jamilah. Generally, I'm the friendly one, drinking generously, dancing around the room, and making friends with strangers. But on this particular night, a semifamiliar face appeared while I was waiting in line for the bathroom. A friend of a friend, whom I might have stalked on Instagram because she was the only other person I knew of with a baby, @watcherica seemed to be living out all of my life goals—complete with a big rock and an engagement to an African prince. I later learned it was mostly all make-believe, because, well, Instagram is a lie. Anyway, here she was cornering me in the club, insisting on a playdate for our daughters. I played it cool, but inside I was geeked up. I hadn't made a new friend in years and certainly none who had any kids. It's rare that the people you stalk on IG become your real-life friends, but, in that moment, my own little fairy tale that I hadn't even known I needed had its beginnings.

ERICA

Hola, I'm Erica—E to a few—a big-hair, don't-care (but I really do), sensitive-ass Scorpio. Instagram brought me to Jamilah, a.k.a. @milah_mapp, and I forced her to be my friend one night in Hollywood. I was three months into motherhood, with no mommy friends, and on my way toward a major breakup I never saw coming. At first, Jamilah and I were friends who got the kids together and didn't dig too deep. It's easy to do that when you have little ones and hundreds of things to complain about. But then at some point in the course of our occasional hangouts, I became single. Let's just keep it one hundred since that is what this book is all about. The reality is my fiancé got another woman pregnant and left me with the hard realization that my dream of being happily married with children wasn't going to happen. My worst fear had come to pass: being a single mom. I had been loyal to someone who treated monogamy like a part-time job. So, after a lot of ugly crying, by myself and with friends, I did what any grieving ex-fiancée would do: I joined Tinder.

MILAH AND ERICA

Soon, our mommy dates turned from superficial vent sessions into real conversations about what it was like to raise a child as a single Black mother who also liked to go out, have fun, and make "questionable choices." Nothing was off-limits between us, and we knew that if we could relate to each other's experiences so easily, there had to be other women who felt the same.

We like to say that a dating app, a threesome, and lots of oversharing led to the birth of our podcast, *Good Moms Bad Choices*, but we know it was a lot more than that. *Good Moms Bad Choices* has been our journey of self-discovery, the foundation of our unexpected sisterhood, and the way we connect with women around the world who are also looking to feel seen and heard by someone who's just as imperfect as they are.

When we started our podcast in 2018, we never could have imagined that it would grow into the platform we've cultivated today. *Good Moms Bad Choices* has been downloaded millions of times and has featured a spectrum of influential voices. From asking social activist Shaun King, "Boxers or briefs?" to requesting the details of a porn star's birth story, we consider no guest or subject off-limits. Our listeners have accompanied us on some of the most painful parts of our journeys as women and mothers, and we have provided a safe space for them to do the same.

The reason we've grown such a loyal following is simple: there is no one else like us in this space today. We are uncensored, cannabis- and sex-positive, single mothers. You won't find us on the mommy blog circuit, either. In fact, we challenge the stereotypes of single parenting and what makes a "good" mother. Our open-book, no-bullshit storytelling combined with our eclectic roster of guests is what keeps listeners coming back for more every week. Serving up a full glass of entertainment and soul-activating topics, *Good Moms Bad Choices* is the support group you never knew you needed. Together, we navigate life's lessons in motherhood, love, spirituality, and sex, with our audience in the passenger seat.

Though neither of our romantic paths played out the way we'd hoped, the two of us ended up with something even better: each other. What started out as casual mommy dates became an incredible friendship that gave us both an undeniable outlet to vent, learn, and connect. Over the past five years we've accepted that good moms make bad choices, too—and that's what makes us human. Being a multidimensional sexual being is good, and you don't have to completely lose who you once were before parenthood to be a great mom.

Today, our imperfect, unapologetic version of motherhood has inspired other mothers and women to rethink what they've been programmed to believe and adopt their own style of motherhood—because, let's face it, no two moms are made the same. Together, we have created the *Good Moms Bad Choices* community, which includes millions of women who have tuned into our audio diary to listen and learn from our journey of redefining modern motherhood. This book is a more in-depth perspective on our individual paths than you'll find on our weekly podcast. Because storytelling is a radical way of creating community and healing, the book is a memoir of sorts, which we hope will also give you advice, guidance, and the confirmation that you are not just a good mom but a great mom, despite your inevitable fuckups.

So, first things first. You should know that the ways each of us navigates motherhood and womanhood are different. The two of us of course share commonalities, but our differences have been crucial in the development of our friendship and partnership. Certain lessons are more important to us as individuals than as friends raising and guiding humans. The ways we parent are inevitably different because of our very different experiences with trauma, relationships, and of course our childhood. We don't always agree on our versions of motherhood, but we also don't judge each other's. It's not our job to judge each other or any other mother. We are all just doing the best we can with the resources we have. Luckily for us, we have a lot of resources, and now you do, too!

As valuable as our unique differences are, there is also something beautiful about what we all share as mothers. We all come into parenthood carrying something from how we were parented: the way we were nurtured as children has directly affected the way we show up as adults and parents. So this book starts with our beginnings. It is organized into three parts: BC (Before Children), AD (After Daddy), and A Rebelation. Our hope is to liberate all moms from the binaries of good and bad and, ultimately, to help us heal past wounds that prevent us from being our best selves as people and as parents.

Please understand when reading this book that we are by no

means claiming to be experts in motherhood or parenting. In fact, on our weekly podcast we openly share all our bad choices and our hope that acknowledging them leads to better ones. One thing is for sure: we all fuck up in different ways, and we've all had fucked-up things happen to us. We are all attempting to sort through our traumas and to dispel beliefs about the world and ourselves that other hurt people have told us. Some of those lies we learned from careless caretakers, teachers, peers, and even family. Many of these "rules" were influenced by religion, culture, environment, and outside forces that intentionally planted moral codes we never had the chance to approve.

Wouldn't the world be a better place if we could all stop pretending we don't fuck up as humans and as parents? How sweet the world could be if we stopped judging other people and shaming others for doing things differently from the way we do things.

What if we took the time to examine the things that didn't serve us in childhood? What if we stopped ignoring and repeating generational traumas by sweeping issues under the rug?

We were told to "stay out of grown folks' business" by people who were having adult conversations in front of kids. We were told to "stop being so fast" because our timeline for exploring our sexuality didn't fit the timeline an adult deemed appropriate.

Whether we're Black, white, purple, or green, we have all seen the damage caused to both parents and children when we ignore difficult topics and avoid uncomfortable conversations. Candid talks about sex, drugs, love, trauma, and relationships are the building blocks to healing and breaking archaic stereotypes. How we choose to inform our children about these topics is how we change the world. In this book, we will explore all of these topics, including our own personal journeys to becoming good moms who make bad choices.

So, who is a good mom who makes bad choices, you ask?

You. Yes, *you*.

Now before you disagree and decide that this book isn't for you, let me ask you something: What defines a good mom? What defines a bad choice?

A mom who goes to every PTA meeting . . . but pops a pill on the car ride home?

A mom who smokes weed . . . but shows up ready to play Barbies like a fucking pro?

A working mom whose career is flourishing . . . but who sometimes struggles to find balance with her children?

Or a mom who lives and dies by her children's every breath . . . and who is miserable in her marriage and has no identity outside of her children?

This book is for all these women—because the moment we stop judging one another is the moment we stop judging ourselves and can begin making better choices. No matter where you are in your life, it's safe to say that this motherhood shit does not come with a handbook. I am not better than you, and you are not better than me. Let's make this an affirmation not only for ourselves, but also for our kids. We were women before we were moms, and until we get that part figured out, how can we possibly show up for our kids?

So how did we become two good moms who have made some bad choices?

Well, let's start from the beginning . . .

Part 1

BC
(BEFORE CHILDREN)

CHAPTER 1

PARENTAL
Advisory

In order to heal the person you want to become, you have to go back to the beginning. Healing your inner child is the first step in changing the trajectory of your life. Whether you grew up in a two-parent household or are the product of a single parent, you have a responsibility to face the parts of your life that created patterns in how you show up as an adult.

ERICA

I never wanted to be a mom. That's not a popular statement among women, but in my case, it's true. I was that person who asked the flight attendant to move me if little Timmy with the snotty nose was my seatmate. Kids were cute, but I couldn't wait to grow up. Once I did, my interest in childish things disappeared. Definitely don't ask me to play. That was my stance, and to be honest, I still don't like to play. Weed helps. We'll get into that later.

Let's just admit it. Say it with me: children are scary AF. I wore my "no kids" badge proudly. My parents' relationship was less than stellar, and my father's absence during my formative years left me in no rush to repeat the same scenario. I was a sensitive child who didn't know how to share that my father's truancy

A GOOD MOM'S GUIDE TO MAKING BAD CHOICES

deeply pained me, that my mother's fast-paced career made me feel I had to be more mature than I was ready to be, or that being one of the only Black kids in my class created an awkward insecurity in both Black and white spaces. Luckily, my mom and her diverse and colorful group of friends offered me a wide perspective of what the world was made of—my first tribe.

She was a celebrity makeup artist, and she brought me on set whenever she could. My superwoman mama taught my intro to Women Create Our Own Destiny 101. But being a superwoman requires hard work, dedication, and time away. When you're a single mom with no real coparent, all that can feel impossible. But you do it—and she did. So there I was, under her makeup chair, entertaining myself at the feet of some of Hollywood's biggest future stars, without a fucking clue. I loved watching her transform her clients into their characters, watching these actors become who they were hired to be. I marveled at them running lines in the mirror or with their castmates while my mom artfully turned them into the characters she saw in them. I took note of the detailed way she created positive experiences for her clients. My Libra mother, the ultimate nurturer.

Mama had to have a life, too. She was a single parent doing the best she could, following her dreams and also looking for love. You can't do all of that with a child on your hip. I spent a lot of time with my grandparents, the nanny, and alone. Thank

God for that time because it gave my creative spirit and mind space to run wild. My imagination took me away. I would daydream in my room and act out the performances of my favorite movies. I learned how to use my imagination and love of performing to hide the hurt I felt about not having my daddy around. My mother did eventually find love, and I had a positive male figure in my home starting around age nine. However, as much as I loved him, he didn't replace my father and the role he was meant to play. I acted out in various ways: gave my mom a hard time, cried at the very mention of my father's name, and looked to boys to give me love. Hello, daddy issues.

I'm going to tell you more about the history of me, because how else can you know how I became a mom who makes bad choices? It's a known fact that childhood and the shit that happens during those years largely influence who we are as functioning —or semifunctioning—adults. What I've learned is that to stop hurting yourself and other people with your questionable choices, it's imperative to go back to the beginning, to double-check and triple-check your traumas, and to reparent yourself, so you can change how you show up in the present. This New Age concept of "reparenting yourself" isn't actually new at all. It's just a fancy way to describe doing the work of being a better human, which often becomes more urgent once you have pushed life into the world. You start to ask yourself questions: *Why do I keep making the same mistakes? How did I end up here?* Unpacking how we were nurtured and how we journeyed to adulthood is the fastest way to find the answers to these questions and not fuck up our kids—even the kids we thought we didn't want. At least, I think so.

What I do know for sure is that having a child of my own has vastly changed my perspective on how my parents navigated parenting me. They were kids, twenty-six years old—babies having a baby. My conception happened during the 1980s in Los Angeles, while my NFL-playing future dad was at the height of his career. One night, he went to a club where his friend Rick James (yup, that one) introduced him to a lady friend who was just as "square" as my clean-cut future dad. The two of them dated and got pregnant, and in no time the football groupies made sure to convince my future dad that he was ruining his life. He left my mom pregnant and questioned whether I was his child. This is where we cue in the public paternity test, lawyers, resentment, and not having a real memory of my father until I was five years old. Even when he showed up in my life, he did so inconsistently. By no means was his 10 percent presence enough to nurture a little girl the way she needs to be nurtured by her first love. She needs her father to show up—to keep his word, teach her, guide her, validate her before she looks to boys for that. Now, as a thirty-something-year-old mother who's been through therapy, gotten the apology from Dad, and actively worked on forgiving him, I can report that our relationship is better than I could have imagined.

But we're not here to talk about the healing. We'll get to that part. We're here to discuss why I never once romanticized having children and why it's my parents' fault. I mean, isn't everything? I kid, I kid. But seriously, how I was parented has everything to do with the woman and mother I am: one with endless resources, thanks to our community of seasoned mothers who have given me permission to think outside the box when it comes to how I love, support, and prepare my daughter for the world. I am a mother with the hyperawareness that my child is not my Mini-Me; she is her own little universe walking around, and I have to respect her will, wishes, and soul path. Even more important, I'm a mother with the hyperawareness that my traumas don't have to be my daughter's, no matter how similar my situation is to my mother's introduction to single motherhood.

When I was a twenty-something-year-old, I had no concept of these ideas yet. I just knew I would never want to have a child and risk her feeling unsupported by her father, the way I had felt. Besides, why would I want to work twice as hard to be the father, mother, and provider if shit hit the fan? Sounds like a drag.

By the time I was a teenager, the traumas from my absent father manifested themselves in an early interest in "adult" things. I started my period at age eleven, and my body quickly matured. I was getting attention from older boys, and I was being exposed to alcohol and talk of blow jobs at my private middle school. I had a lot of questions and feelings. I felt embarrassed asking about my body and the attention it was getting, so I did what most of us did and relied on other stupid teenagers for my education in sexuality. Yup, because a prepubescent teen totally knows how to make it all make sense. A delicate mixture of nature, bad advice, rom-coms, no daddy around, and a very busy first-time mommy led me to seek attention and value through my above-average interest in the opposite sex.

I've always been independent as a free-spirited, feisty Scorpio —a rebel, if you will. Okay, fine—a rebel with anxiety. I truly believe my innate intuitiveness and a healthy dose of rationality kept me alive during my incredibly irresponsible teenage years, with all my bad choices. This rebellion was, of course, the source of the contentious relationship between me and my mother then, but it also deeply defines who I am right now. If you asked my tribe, meaning my friends and family, they would probably describe me as opinionated, sensitive, protective, and caring, with a healthy dose of IDGAF. We will get into that later on in the book, because I actually used to give a lot of fucks—too many fucks. I was just great at disguising my deep insecurities with a confident front.

As I said before, I was a mature child; my body caught up rather quickly, and boys and men noticed. Blame Sisqó, my dad's extensive *Playboy* collection, the unlimited porn channels at my best friend's house, or good ole daddy issues. According to my very detailed diary, I had my first crush at seven, started hating girls who liked my crushes at nine, and began thinking about sex at eleven. Two years later I lost my virginity, and my obsession with love and attention from the opposite sex was ignited.

It happened in my backyard. Well, technically, we were in the shed in the backyard. Either way, it was not sexy and not what any parent hopes for a daughter's first time. Kyle went to the all-boys prep school behind my house. He was beautiful. Cornrows, caramel skin, and his big, sleepy, light eyes locked me in. He played basketball, and his athletic build made my teenage heart pitter-patter. He asked for my number, and I wrote it down on a piece of paper without hesitation. I knew what I wanted, and this newfound interest in Kyle felt exciting and naughty. He was older, mature, the sixteen-year-old of my dreams. I knew he would be the one to make me a "woman." We hung out secretly after school, and I snuck him into my house while my mom was at work. We messed around until a few days later, he asked if

I was a virgin. I told him yes, and I saw his eyes light up. I felt special—like I had a special gift and I wanted him to have it—to own it, to take care of it, and me.

The next day I snuck him into my backyard. He kissed me romantically, picked me up, and placed me on the edge of a table in my parents' dusty toolshed. He put a condom on, the first time I had ever seen one outside of its packaging. He pulled down my shorts and pressed into me. I felt a sharp pain until I didn't anymore. Five or six strokes later, it was over. I remember thinking, *That wasn't that bad*, and also that it wasn't as romantic as I had imagined it would be. I lost my virginity on top of a dirty table in my dusty garage. I was in love. He wasn't. He also wasn't convinced I was a virgin because I didn't bleed and because, apparently, I seemed "experienced." I was concerned and flattered all at once. Was there something wrong with my vagina? Why didn't I bleed? Was it broken?

I didn't dare ask my mother. She was already stressed enough with a new baby, and I had no toolbox for how to even approach that conversation. I'm also sure my mom wasn't anticipating me losing my virginity at thirteen in her dirty shed. Sorry, Mom.

My virginity popper was a ho. He didn't understand how momentous an occasion this was for me. Neither did I. My actual boyfriend found out I cheated on him, and I was left boyfriendless and no longer a virgin. With questions about whether my pussy was broken and whether sex was something worth covenanting, I spiraled into a promiscuous cycle of meaningless sexual interactions with a mix of serial relationships and excessive cheating. The moment I departed from one guy, I needed to find someone else to love me. Enter baby daddy; let's call him BD for short.

> ## Affirmation
> I am not the trauma or cycles of my childhood, my parents, their parents, or their belief systems. I am not obligated to carry their guilt, shame, or unhappiness.

I met him at the top of the Standard Hotel in downtown Los Angeles. I was twenty-two and on a date with my summer fling looking for weed. My friend told me she knew a guy and that he was coming to the party. "Yes!" As I sat in the waterbed dome by the pool (if you know, you know) and took pictures with the love of my life of the month, suddenly out of nowhere appeared a tall, slim-faced man with a XXL white tee and charismatic sleepy eyes. Baby was a thug.

"Hey, your girl told me you were looking for tree."

Sure was.

I bought the weed, took his number because reliable drug dealers in the Valley were hard to come by, and carried on eye-gazing at my future overseas-basketball-player husband. Little did I know that the guy with oversize clothes and a sweet disposition would be the father of my future child I never thought I wanted.

We were platonic friends for a year. I had gotten back together with my semiabusive ex after basketball bae went back to Germany, because that's what love addicts do. But I still found time to hang out with future BD because he was funny, sweet, and gave me free weed. He never flirted with me or made me feel uncomfortable, which was a relief. He felt safe, and I was happy to have a platonic male friend for once. After a year of secret smoke sessions and a final breakup, I went to New York for work, and BD happened to be there too. Before I knew it, we linked up, we got drunk, and we had sweaty, unexpected sex for six hours straight. My homie quickly became my lover and best friend. We moved in six months into dating and loved each other without a single disagreement for two years. I never had even the slightest urge to seek attention elsewhere. I was fulfilled and convinced this imperfect human was my soulmate. I still believe he is. I also believe we have more than one soulmate; I have to. Cue Boyz II Men, "Yesterday."

Anyway, that's a whole other book.

Four years in, I found myself unhappy. His music career was growing, and attention from women became too much for him to handle. I was twenty-five and battling with who I was and what I wanted to do with my life. I just knew that by my midtwenties I should have my shit together, and I didn't. I had been acting most of my life without any huge breaks and writing music and singing without landing my dream record deal. Serving tables was my side hustle, and I fucking hated it. I felt creatively inept as I saw my partner flow with ideas like a machine. It was beautiful to watch him totally aligned with his purpose. Witnessing his drive and relentlessness lent much to my becoming the creative entrepreneur I am today. I traveled with him on tour and got very comfortable avoiding myself by pouring all my love and support into BD, even when he didn't deserve it—because for some odd reason, that's what women do.

Soon I discovered a burner phone with women in other cities texting my man (baby was a thug), which led to a brief breakup, an abortion, and an abrupt move to NYC. I went there to find myself without him, but New York can be a lonely city. My historic need for love outweighed my desire to love and find myself. I blame the fact that he happened to be the love of my life at the time. I also blame the fact that Tinder didn't exist.

A year later, I found myself back with my soulmate in Jamaica, for a "let's try this again" trip. Bad choice? Maybe, but the rum and punch flowed, my free-spirited flag waved, we had anal sex for the first time, and it rocked my muthafuckin' world. Highly recommend lube, ladies.

When I came back, I was back in love and very much . . . pregnant. Fuck.

MILAH

Long before I became a mom, I was a self-proclaimed "wild woman." Most of my friends voted me the least likely to settle down and didn't even bet on me keeping my first pet alive longer than six weeks.

Despite popular belief, I had secretly always longed for the white picket fence, three children, and a husband. Maybe it was the four hundred Disney movies I had consumed or the thousands of images I'd seen of "successful women" being wed and living happily ever after. Or maybe it was the hope that I'd break all the norms of the stereotypical Black family and "make it," full family intact. After all, my parents "made it"—kind of.

Growing up in the San Fernando Valley, a suburb of Los Angeles, is interesting for a young Black girl. My parents were pro-Black AF, but navigating among primarily white and oftentimes oblivious peers was confusing, yet became oddly normal to me.

As a teenager, I was aware of who I was and even more aware that nobody could really tell me differently—not my parents, not my teachers, not my closest friends. I was wildly curious and had little fear. Looking back, I now know that part of my personality came from a combination of genetics and watching my mother quietly suffer as a sacrifice for her high school sweetheart and two children.

My parents, both Philadelphia natives, started dating when my dad was seventeen and my mom was fourteen. They were babies when they met on the L train in inner-city Philly. They weren't much older when they migrated together to Montgomery, Alabama, where they attended the HBCU Tuskegee University and would eventually conceive and birth me at the tender ages of twenty-two and twenty-five. Eventually, my mom managed to graduate despite the odds, and we all ended up in Los Angeles when my dad followed his dream of becoming a writer with a childhood friend on a show called *The Fresh Prince of Bel-Air*.

Growing up I was always pretty easygoing, making peace and not war and careful not to take up too much space; after all, I was a child, and children had to stay in their place. But I've always been opinionated and unafraid to share my perspective. I vividly remember when I was six, maybe seven, sitting across from my mother at our dining room table, looking at her and feeling her sadness, and simply asking her, "Why don't you leave him?" I was talking about my father. Even at that age, I was fully aware of the turmoil and conflict brewing in my household on a regular basis. Although I was young, I had an immense amount of common sense, as I believe a lot of children do in the beginning stages of life. It's almost as if the older we get, the further we get from our intuition. I was mature and the only child among all adults, but being a deeply sensitive human allowed me to be highly receptive to the energies of others. I had already overheard too many fights and arguments about other women and had witnessed my dad not come home many nights only for my mom to meet him in a rage many mornings.

Being an only child for quite some time subconsciously made me adopt this idea that I shouldn't be heard or seen. I did my best to blend in, until there was a turning point. One day in middle school, a random girl decided she wanted to fight me. Having been slightly sheltered in suburbia, with the exception of my summer trips to visit my cousins in Philly, I had witnessed only two or three school brawls, which had shaken up my young, sensitive, Cancerian world. But on this day, a crowd of peers stormed into my classroom to alert me that I was scheduled to fight in the parking lot across the street after school. I was terrified, sweating profusely, and riddled with butterflies of anxiety. I vividly recall noon approaching, the school bell ringing, and the fear in the pit of my stomach growing. I had a moment of dialogue with myself and discovered my inner voice: *You have two choices—chicken out or fight.*

At that moment I hadn't realized yet, but I'd later understand, that fear was a choice. Giving a fuck was a choice, and I had too much pride and far too much Philly in my DNA to ever publicly turn down a fight—or any challenge that came my way, for that matter. There and then, at twelve years old, I became aware of the conscious choice between being afraid when unforeseen challenges came my way or facing them head-on like the boss-ass bitch that I was. I realized then that we all have a little fear and we all have a little fight, and it was up to us to pour into either well for fruition. The girl never actually came to fight me that day in the parking lot, but I will never forget the covenant I made with myself and how quickly the physical fear in my body dissipated once I decided not to be scared. Even though the fight itself turned out to be a nonevent, the decision I made to fight set a tone for my life and a standard for myself that led me to say, "Fuck it. Let's see what happens."

As time progressed, this newfound fearlessness, paired with my teenage hormones, caused me to dive headfirst into boys and bullshit. My parents' infatuation with each other made them more occupied than available, and I, of course, took advantage of that. No slight to them; I now understand, as a parent, that this shit doesn't come with a blueprint. But I had too much time on my hands, and they were too occupied to notice.

By the time I was thirteen, I was at my second private school. I was bored as hell and ready to indulge in anything remotely tantalizing. There were zero attractive boys at Valley School, and my childhood tomboy crush, Asia, was my classmate, along with a handful of horny badass preteen girls. Somewhere along the way one of them got their hands on a book about two emo, white, teenage bitches who cut themselves; drank vodka in water bottles at school; and did a bunch of rebellious, sexual, and lesbian stupid shit for attention. So guess what we did after passing around the book? We mimicked every fucking stupid-ass thing in the stupid-ass book. We even one-upped the book's characters: we added using computer cleaner as a recreational drug and shoplifting.

Again, the danger of bored teenage girls is inexplicable, and as I write this for all to dissect, I cringe and smile at the same time. Was this a traditional "rough patch" for a thirteen-year-old girl? Probably not for most—but for a Valley girl? Probably.

By the time I made it out of the Valley School, I was fully aware that I had the capacity to simply love people and be attracted to both guys and girls. I had graduated from huffing computer cleaner after school and ended my lesbian phase, turning instead to sneaking boys into my room after football games and dry humping till the wee hours of the morning. Of course, I eventually got caught sneaking boys in, got my ass whooped, was put on punishment for what felt like hundreds of months, eventually became "saved," joined a Christian youth group, and temporarily sat the fuck down.

About a year into the youth group, I developed an even bigger attraction to my girl crush, Asia, and that caused me to question why God would allow me to be so in love with a girl if he knew it was sinful and "un-Christian." I was later introduced to Buddhism and adopted the practice of chanting. Even early on, I was malleable and curious. I've always genuinely enjoyed exploring the nuances and layers of existing in many ways. I guess you can say that I am by nature a true explorer. I have always been open to discovering new things, people, perspectives, and experiences. Seeking has always been my way of relating to the world around me. This openness has led me to many places in my life and introduced me to even more people. My ability to say yes more than no has served me well. My innocent curiosity has serendipitously led me exactly to places I needed to be, lessons I needed to learn, and humans I needed to know. Growing up, I saw my mom be skeptical and weary of people, so I chose the path of opening and trusting and allowed myself to flow where life wanted to take me.

When I lost my virginity at around thirteen or fourteen, it heightened the kinds of experiences I could have. I discovered dick and was strung out like a crackhead. I started wearing lingerie to school underneath my uniform; taking the bus to see my ninth-grade love; fucking at movie theaters, in dressing rooms, closets, and back seats. At age sixteen, even while exploring my newfound sexuality and my strange relationship with love, I still remained closest to the tall, skinny, brace-faced basketball player from the private school down the road. I met my high school sweetheart at a football game briefly, and then we chatted on AOL Instant Messenger and talked on the phone for months after. At that time, coming across a Black boy in the same age range in the Valley was a rarity. He was tall and had a big, beautiful smile and big, kind eyes.

We were inseparable and spent hours and hours having late-night teenage conversations and falling asleep on the phone, planning our future. He was the first boy I actually told my parents I was dating and the first boy whose house I actually asked if I could visit; my parents brought me there and met his parents. We attended every prom together, went on each other's family vacations, had after-school homework hangouts daily, even worked at the same summer camp. He got his license before me, so he drove me and all my friends to cheer competitions. I attended all his basketball games, and we were allowed to sleep over at each other's houses on the weekends. I got his name tattooed on my ass, then covered it up a few months later when my dad found a receipt. My future baby daddy and I developed a real relationship, and because our parents approved, somehow the relationship felt destined for marriage.

I vividly envisioned our future together, but deep down, something in me was wildly curious about what else the world had to offer. Even though I was deeply in love with my FBD, I also knew I wanted to explore, but I didn't know how to communicate that. Saying you wanted to "explore" was equivalent to admitting you wanted to ho, and no future husband wanted that. At the time, I didn't recognize how much shame the high school standard for teenage girls could breed. The rumors and gossip about who was doing what circulated mostly only about the girls, probably because the boys made the rules and the rumors. It's crazy how shame will have you resenting yourself and hiding who you really are. Instead of being completely honest and just breaking up with FBD, I did what was familiar to me: I lied and sneaked and made excuses for not wanting to spend time with FBD. In all honesty, I broke his heart repeatedly with my actions and lies, mostly because I was riddled with fears of shame and judgment and lacked the tools to comfortably communicate who I was at the time and what I needed.

This is probably why the universe then sent me Boo, a famous porn star, at the peak of my raging hormones. Welcome to the Valley.

Boo was tall, dark chocolate, complete with dimples, beautiful straight white teeth, and impeccable confidence. It was a warm summer day when I met him. In an all-white Maserati, he pulled up on my cousin and me walking down the street, asked for our number, and pulled back off. We later called him and arranged a date for him to pick us up, this time from my parents' house.

When he picked us up, he arrived in a shiny new Range Rover. We scurried into the car because, of course, I was paranoid that my parents would peek out our front window and question who the fuck was picking up their eighteen-year-old daughter in a Range midweek.

Meanwhile, in the car, my eighteen-year-old "mature" yet naive ass was questioning this grown man.

"Do you have a girlfriend?"

"I have a lot of girlfriends. Do you want to be one?" He was grinning from ear to ear.

I had never experienced a grown man deliver such honesty with charm, confidence. I was immediately intrigued and enthralled with my new friend Boo.

That was the first time a man was unapologetically honest with me, and it made my teenage pussy wet. I had witnessed my mom and dad argue over infidelity and lies, and here this sexy stranger was keeping it one hundred. His honesty resonated with me on levels I hadn't recognized needed healing. I grew up in an environment where people who allegedly loved each other lied and hurt each other. I recognized early on that this couldn't possibly be my destiny.

I can see now that my craze for the opposite sex and my desperate, aimless search for love and attention came from the lack of attention in my household. My parents' relationship was toxic and created in me a disdain for long-term relationships and marriage. I felt my parents struggle in their relationship and witnessed soap-opera-worthy drama play out in my household on a regular basis. I was a hopeless romantic who desperately longed for love while also hating it.

As an adult, dissecting the elements of my childhood and how they've played out in the ways I show up in my relationships and attachment styles has been hard and also deeply enlightening. It's important to recognize that you don't have to grow up in an extremely chaotic or abusive household to absorb toxic behaviors. It's also important to recognize how you normalize and sugarcoat these experiences. You may not even register your trauma as trauma. I've found that women are less likely to be aware of the pain they experience because we're so inclined to be strong and "deal with it." Let me be the first to tell you, not acknowledging your own pain is a sure way to personal disaster. You, me, we all deserve to cry. We all deserve to not be strong sometimes. Our feelings are valid, and we're allowed to feel shit and break down, too.

This is your cue to be honest with yourself and recognize traumatic events in your life, to begin healing from them. List some things that have happened to you or messages you've heard that may be affecting the way you love yourself and others. Get in the trenches with your trauma, so you can begin the process of releasing it.

My relationship with Boo wasn't sustainable, but meeting him ignited a freedom in me that I had suppressed with FBD. As I packed up for college, I was sad to leave FBD but equally excited to embrace this new version of myself, away from him and away from my family. I had to break away from my household, which housed years and years of emotional turmoil in my parents' toxic-ass relationship, and I was ready to see what life had to offer me. Looking back, I was running, because that was the only solution I knew. Healing for me meant running as far away from home as possible.

My life in Atlanta was a whirlwind. I went through an OD ho phase and before that, I even managed to get in three years of full-on monogamous lesbian relationships that I hadn't foreseen. Eventually, though, my life in Atlanta became repetitive; working as a cocktail waitress in a city that never sleeps and being a bitch who never says no can become problematic.

Eventually, it dawned on me at twenty-four that being a professional cocktail waitress wasn't going to be my be-all and end-all. Even in the midst of my party lifestyle, I knew I was ready for change, and change would not come as long as I stayed in Atlanta. When I finally made the decision to return home, I was disappointed in myself. I hadn't finished my degree; I had been under the impression that my parents would be funding my tuition, and when that didn't happen, work took the front seat and education came in last. I felt as though I had spent those seven years BSing and learning the art of waitressing, which would only get me more waitressing work. I moved back in with my mom and dad, and they seemed even more dysfunctional than they had been when I left. I checked in from time to time, but I had been living on my own for years, and this was by no means a permanent situation.

So I jumped back into what seemed most familiar: my relationship with FBD. His NBA dreams hadn't come to fruition, and he was seeing a popular video model and living with his parents; but I was determined to get him back. Sure enough, where there's a will, there's a way. I got my man back; I started working random jobs, and eventually we moved in together and resumed where we had left off—except we weren't the same people anymore, and we were no longer in high school. I had moved away and lived on my own; I had grown up in a lot of ways, and he still had not. Nevertheless, I settled into what was familiar, and within a year of living together my period was late—really late.

A Visit to Your Inner Child

Take a moment alone to revisit your inner child by envisioning your childhood home. Visualize your younger self and comfort her. Find the words you wish someone had said to you and say those words to yourself.

CHAPTER 2

FUCK, I'm Expecting

Pregnancy can be triggering, beautiful, and isolating. Confusing, right? The shifts in your body, identity, and friendships can feel overwhelming. On the other hand, the life growing inside of you plants seeds of self-advocacy and intuition that you may not have experienced before. Pregnancy is a very real understanding that nothing will ever be the same again.

ERICA

When I saw the two lines appear across all three drugstore pregnancy tests, tears welled up in my eyes. I was alone in my baby daddy's bedroom. He was out of town, and I was staying at his place in LA during one of my extended visits. We hadn't declared that we were back together, but Jamaica had confirmed that we weren't done, and so did the three plastic pee sticks sitting on the bathroom counter. I was in love—the kind of love that you know is once in a lifetime, even if it isn't perfect. Forever was exactly what I wanted, the family dynamic I never got to see with my parents. "Break generational curses," they say. But at what cost?

I weighed the good and bad, because although I was happy, I was still scared as shit.

> ## Affirmation
> **My body has been given the incredible gift to be a vessel for life. I joyfully accept the challenges and changes that come with this soul-shifting privilege.**

I want to be clear for those reading this who aren't parents yet and those who are considering having kids or feeling pressured to do so. Just to put it plainly: motherhood is not a requirement.

ERICA'S SHOULD-I-HAVE-A-BABY-WITH-THIS-PERSON CHECKLIST

BAD CHOICES	GOOD CHOICES
☐ We technically weren't back together	☐ I loved him
☐ I still lived in New York	☐ I loved him
☐ I was broke	☐ I loved him
☐ My mother wasn't his biggest fan	☐ I loved him
☐ I wasn't sure he could be faithful	☐ I loved him
☐ I had no friends with kids	☐ I felt he'd be a great father
☐ I didn't want kids	☐ We had been together for 5 years and . . . well that's a long time when you're 26

This mommy life stuff isn't "cute" all the time, no matter how much society and media portray it to be. Motherhood will not make your relationship stronger and will not make your partner or family take you more seriously. In fact, motherhood will test all your relationships, especially your romantic one.

When you are a mother, anything that annoys you now will be intensified, and anything that your partner didn't do before, he or she will probably still not do. To put it frankly, just because your partner picks up babies at parties and plays with them for fifteen minutes doesn't mean your partner will be a great parent.

Based on my checklist, one would clearly see that the odds of this being easy weren't exactly in my favor. I was naive. I could have waited, and things might have been easier, but who knows where I'd be? I most definitely wouldn't be writing this book and building an epic community with my best friend, Jamilah. Everyone who decides to have a baby is a little naive, no matter how old they are. Some are better equipped than I was, but you just don't know what you've signed up for until you do it.

All I knew was that my mind was made up—that my life-long vow to never have kids was trumped by love and the tiny seed growing inside me. Even my fear of telling my mom and her inevitable judgment wouldn't sway me. Nope, not this time. This was a big-girl decision, and I was ready to make it. Call it intuition, daddy issues, or a woman's ever-evolving capacity to handle shit, but I knew that whatever happened, we would be okay. We were having a baby, and I was filled with immense joy and purpose.

I moved back to LA, and we moved into a little house in the San Fernando Valley, where I grew up. Yes, I am an Afro Latina girl from the Valley who's equal parts "Like, oh my gaaawd" and "Nigga what?" The Valley is also where my mom lived, and I hoped that moving closer to her and showing her we were a "real family" would help ease her mind and make me feel better about my "bad choices." She saw my checklist without having to see my checklist. Moms be knowin', and I'm sure she saw herself in me as I decided to change my life forever. She wasn't a fan of my decision, and I wasn't a fan of her opinion. However, in the words of my mother herself, "time is the greatest neutralizer," and in time she came to accept and get excited for the arrival of her firstborn glam baby.

My pregnancy was going well, and my partner was holding up his side of the deal. He rubbed my feet, attended every doctor's appointment, marveled at my changing body, took care of the bills, and was elated at the idea of being a father—us being a family. I watched a million birth videos, bought *What to Expect When You're Expecting*, researched baby shit till my eyes rolled back, and began nesting like a maniac in our new little home. I avoided all the things they say you have to avoid or you're a bad mom: sushi, uncured meats and cheese, alcohol, and weed. I followed my doctor's orders to a T out of fear that I could possibly harm this child with my old ways and habits. Prior to pregnancy I was a heavy smoker. No, not cigarettes. Mary Jane is my choice of herb, which is fitting considering that the legend himself introduced my parents. I began smoking at thirteen, and cannabis had been a staple in my everyday life. It made me balanced and . . . hungry. But Google and my family told me cannabis was dangerous, so that was out, too. If there is one thing I've learned since then it's that Google, although helpful, is filled with tons of misinformation, and so are friends and family. They mean well, but do your due diligence and fact-check everything. With that said, make your own choices when it comes to cannabis, and keep reading to find out about Jamilah's experience with the flower and pregnancy. If I knew then what I know now, I would have maybe used cannabis to ease my nausea, pain, and anxiety throughout my pregnancy.

Aside from that misinformation and judgment around the use of cannabis, when it came to making my birth plan, I was totally clear on what I wanted—or so I thought. My friend told me to watch *The Business of Being Born*, a wonderful film by Ricki Lake, and I learned about the unnecessary interventions hospitals and the health-care system force upon mothers and their babies, from the high induction rate for the sake of making beds available to the classic hospital "lithotomy" position, with a woman lying on her back and being instructed to push, even though this position is proven to make her pelvis smaller. What I learned and my intuition really made me rethink giving birth the traditional way. I decided outwardly and inwardly that a natural home birth was what I wanted.

When I broke the news to future baby daddy, he was hesitant. This was his first child, and a home birth sounded scary and risky. When I told my family and friends, they had a similar reaction. I was asked, "Why?" and "Are you sure?" I was, and I explained that Ricki Lake said it was the best thing to do and so did the dozens of home-birth videos I had watched. I told my ob-gyn last. As we walked into her luxury office at Cedars-Sinai

I felt excited to share the news with her. I knew she—another woman, who had children and had delivered thousands of babies—would understand and support me.

"Do you know how many dead home-birth babies I've delivered?"

Fuck. I was wrong.

I felt the judgment in her voice and the fear that I was selfishly putting my daughter's life at risk for an "experience." My intuition really made me rethink giving birth the traditional way, but my doctor's energy around my grand idea instantly made me feel uneasy. I was treading in uncharted territory and wanted to make the best decision. Looking back, I realize how silly it was to bring this idea to her. I was looking for her validation while also telling her that her role in the process would be diminished.

Hey, Doc, sooo I think I won't really be needing you cuz I'm doing this at home. So, say goodbye to the thousands you'll surely make off my body and my baby's grand entrance.

Yeah, dumb.

But I was high off YouTube and Ricki Lake, and I was excited to tell my fellow female and mama doctor that I had made an executive decision to trust and have autonomy over my body. She wasn't having it. She told me that I was being irresponsible with my firstborn child—that I should see how I felt the first time, and maybe baby number two would be my miracle home-birth experience. Baby daddy shook his head in agreement, and I was filled with guilt and apprehension. Was I being irresponsible? Was my twenty-seven-year-old body not capable of pushing a baby out the way God intended? Was I going to kill my baby with my hippie-dippie mentality? My Beverly Hills celebrity doctor seemed to think so, and I had zero friends with kids and therefore no recent blueprint to lean on. My family are "go to the doctor" people, so they were relieved when I shared how my appointment went.

That week, in a final attempt to follow my gut, I started researching midwives. Maybe if we spoke to one, it would affirm my intuition and ease baby daddy's reservations. I looked around for a Black doula in Los Angeles. I didn't have much luck on that front. Later in my journey in podcasting, I would learn from Racha Tahani, one of the first Black midwives in Los Angeles, how hard it is for Black women to get the support and education white midwives do, let alone recognition on the internet. I opted for a nice white lady I spoke with on the phone and made an appointment for her to come to our home for a consultation.

Consultation day came, and I came ready with a bunch of questions that I hoped would plead my case that a home birth was right for us. The guilt had continued to linger from my last checkup appointment, and unsolicited advice told me that the baby wasn't just mine and that I needed to be considerate of baby daddy's wishes, too. She ran down what a home birth would look like and what our options were, and then BD asked the question I knew would eventually come.

"So, what happens if something goes wrong?"

I knew what she would say. Shit.

"Then we go to the hospital."

And there you have it: the story of how my set-in-stone birth plan went to shit. Looking back, I see that I really didn't put up a fight the way the Erica I know now would have. I was scared to speak up for myself in an arena I felt I knew nothing about.

I just knew that I wanted everyone to be happy and my baby to be healthy. I thought about me last because I was told that's what I was supposed to do as a mother. Everything was about the health of the baby and not my own needs, wants, desires, or capabilities. This is what they want you to believe so that you succumb to the inevitable cash trap of motherhood. I am here to tell you that your needs absolutely matter—that your intuition is right and that you should, first and foremost, think about yourself. This does not make you a bad mom. It prepares you for the inevitable sacrifices you will have to make as a mother and the onslaught of opinions about your parenting that will surely come your way. You will need to be strong in your body, your health, and who the fuck you are. Losing yourself in self-sacrifice will prolong the journey back to yourself. Start this practice now.

Let's talk about pregnancy and the things I had to learn along the way. Yes, pregnancy was great, but it was also lonely in ways. Nobody tells you that you lose friends. Yup, some of those friends you used to party with, who were your "besties for life"—they leave. You aren't fun anymore. You're kind of embarrassing. Maybe it was my age, or maybe people are just trash. I was twenty-six when I got pregnant, and I quickly noticed how I didn't get invited to the BBQ or even a boozy brunch anymore. I wasn't even showing yet, for God's sake! I had stopped waitressing, and auditioning was off the table, so it was just me, my belly, and whoever decided to come around. Baby daddy told me that he wanted me to just be big, fat, and happy, and he would take care of the rest. He kept his word.

I gained seventy pounds. Yes, seventy motherfucking pounds,

pun intended. Sex and love had turned me into a mother—a big, heavy, stretched-to-the-max mother. My daughter weighed seven pounds, eleven ounces, so this made absolutely no sense. It was my fault. I ate a pint of Ben & Jerry's Half Baked ice cream every other night. I was eating for two, right? I was assured that I would drop the weight during breastfeeding, but nobody told me that breastfeeding could potentially be hard AF or warned me about the tiredness I was about to endure.

I was also told that pregnancy would make me horny. That's a joke. At least it was for me. I was basically asexual, which gave my partner even more reason to stray, unbeknownst to me. They also don't tell you about the shift that happens the moment that baby comes out of your body—the way your partner feels unneeded because he really is useless-ish. In my mind, we were going to do skin-to-skin, and it would be a fifty-fifty parenting situation. Wrong. Baby doesn't want dad because you have liquid gold flowing from your tits and a soft, familiar scent and body. Dads go into "protect and provide" mode, often leaving us mothers alone on the couch pumping for dear life. No one ever told me about the hardship my relationship would go through. Becoming a mother is a transition not just for you, but for your partner and the access they have to you.

It's hard to feel like sucking dick or riding cowgirl when there's an actual human sucking your tit and crying at the very departure of your touch. Some men think post-baby mama you is sexy, and some long for the days their hot wife or girlfriend actually took a shower every day.

Seeing your vagina stretch beyond what you ever thought possible, or seeing your guts lying on the table as I did, is not something that quickly leaves your mind. According to a study, most men's interest in sex decreases after childbirth for many of the reasons just listed, on top of the immense pressure society puts on them to bring back the loot. Oh, and if you weren't super solid in the first place, don't expect pregnancy to be the on switch for your relationship. But motherhood is not all doom and darkness. It does and will get better—promise. This chapter sounds like a prescription for birth control, and maybe it is, but I just want to share the realities of pregnancy. These are not everyone's experiences, but I wish I had known about the darkness beforehand, so that the light would seem brighter and the small wins more like victories.

So, let's talk about our bodies—these beautiful, incredible vessels that house, nurture, and protect our little humans. Before Irie, I struggled with body dysmorphia. On the spectrum of an eating disorder, I was definitely on the lighter end, but I had dabbled in diet pills, extreme diets, overeating, and undereating, and only occasionally was I satisfied with the state of my physical body. Growing up in LA and acting and modeling at a young age definitely did a number on my body confidence. I had a mature figure as a teenager and felt awkward among my white counterparts who could easily squeeze into a pair of Frankie Bs without their whole right ass cheek hanging out. Somewhere along the way, media started to embrace ass (hello, J.Lo!) and I started to, sort of, embrace what my mama gave me. As my body started to change during the first three months of pregnancy, I started feeling triggered by my old feelings that I looked fat. If you've been pregnant, then you know that awkward beginning period, when you don't look "with child," but you do look as though you'd just eaten an extra-large pepperoni pizza, heavy on the salt. Between being beyond exhausted—because my body was working overtime laying the foundation of a human—and having my skin break out and morning sickness, I felt that my body was betraying me. Where the fuck was my glow?

Four months in, I was starting to feel more normal, or maybe I was just getting used to this new existence. I went over to the house of a friend who happened to be a photographer. She had just moved in and wanted to show me her rooftop.

"Let me take a few pictures of you?" she asked.

"Sure," I said.

I posed as she snapped photos of me against the sunset. I felt awkward as I cradled my bloated belly. When she showed me the pictures, my mouth dropped.

"Holy shit."

"What?" she asked in confusion.

"I'm pregnant."

"Duh!"

They say that one day, you look up, and suddenly you have a belly. Well, it's true. I couldn't believe how my body had changed without me noticing. So, there I was, four months preggo, belly poppin', and I finally felt cute AF. I embraced my new bump and wore every item of spandex clothing I could find to show off my belly and this booty at the same damn time.

Once I had fully accepted that I was pregnant, I also told myself that I could finally eat everything I wanted without shame. I had been on diets most of my life, but this belly was the mask to all my overeating and the stress-bingeing that would ensue. At my six-month checkup, I had gained thirty pounds, and my doctor advised me to watch my diet. I didn't listen, and I would pay the price later. For now, Ben and Jerry's was keeping me warm while BD was out of town or working late. As my pregnancy progressed, I felt the spark in my relationship diminish. I wasn't interested in going out, having sex, smoking, or partaking in the "childish" activities I had loved before. I was in full-blown nesting mode. All the baby books I read, other expecting moms I met, and everything I consumed on TV caused my mind to shift and made me feel more conservative and traditional. The internet said that this baby was now my entire life and it was time to grow up and be a mature adult. All these people laid it on thick, and I became a full-blown bore. My relationship suffered as a result.

I overate and worried about what my life would look like after pregnancy. At my nine-month checkup, I was 220 pounds, and every part of my body ached. I felt like a cow, and I wished I had been more active or health-conscious over the preceding few months. Instead, I refused to work out and used food and reality TV as a temporary band-aid for my lingering depression. If I ever have another child I would make my physical health a priority. Staying active is nonnegotiable if you want to "bounce back"—unless you're Jamilah, who's ninety-eight pounds soaking wet. A quick bounce back is not most people's reality and certainly wasn't mine. The moral of the story is to try to stay active during pregnancy, and talk nice to your body from beginning to end. Try with all your might! This effort will help keep your mind, body, and spirit in healthy balance.

The Five-Second Test

G rab a piece of paper and a pen, or start a note on your phone. Write down one thing about your body that you currently love or want to begin loving. Make something up if you have to. Once you've written it down, read your note out loud. Do this now, before reading any further.

Okay, so ask yourself how long it took to recall or decide what you'd choose. Be honest.

Thirty seconds? Five minutes? A whole twenty-four hours?

So now I want you to put this note where you can easily access it: your wallet, the mirror in the bathroom, your phone screensaver. Read this note out loud, repeatedly, every day for thirty days. Try it out in the mirror; recite it while you're at the gym, driving, applying lotion to your gorgeous body. Physical action behind an affirmation is proven to create new neural pathways in your brain—much like the ones we have created by talking shit to ourselves all day. If there is one thing I want you to know, it's how important it is for you to be able to recall out loud the work you're doing on healing and loving yourself. It shouldn't take more than five seconds if you're really working on it. Keep it short, like mine:

I love my stomach. Jiggly or firm, it is sexy and beautiful.

As my due date got closer, I gazed in the mirror at myself and couldn't wait for pregnancy to be over. I was ready to take back ownership of my body and meet my child. I was ready to have my little perfect family. I was hopeful that once she was here, my relationship would restore itself; that after hours of watching YouTube and Kourtney Kardashian pull her baby out of herself (literally), I could have a natural drug-free birth; and that my beautiful newborn baby girl would enter the world by way of my capable yoni and crawl up to my titty the way motherfucking nature designed.

Boy, was I wrong.

MILAH

To keep it completely one hundred the weeks leading up to my pregnancy, my FBD and I were living it up in our scantily furnished apartment, hosting impromptu house parties that may or may not have been accompanied by a hell of a lot of Jameson and cocaine. As you can imagine, this is how I became knocked up at twenty-six. I honestly started to believe he just couldn't get me pregnant, and I got too comfortable and almost fond of letting him cum inside me. Romanticizing a family during climax was kinky and amplified our orgasms. In hindsight, I got pregnant because (1) I was dumb AF and irresponsible AF; and (2) the part of my life that overflowed with debauchery needed to come to an end, and Spirit had her own way of bidding farewell. A transition was taking place, and a shift that I didn't know I needed was taking the driver's seat, a message from the universe

> ## Affirmation
> **I am divinely guided, and I trust my body and my intuition.**

if you will. The first domino in a row of millions had fallen. Even though I moved back home to find some normalcy instead of the wild life I was living in Atlanta, the wild life was alive and well and following me. It wasn't long before I realized FBD hadn't really gotten his full "party mode" out yet the way I had, and he liked drinking and fucking even more than I did.

Many may read this, immediately clutch their pearls, and think, *I'm putting this book down. What kind of woman, let alone mother, would openly admit that the series of events that led to her little pumpkin's conception consisted of such debauchery?* But before you put this book down, having decided that you and I are completely different people, I will be the first to tell you: We absolutely are. All women—all people—are different. In fact, the moral of this story is that no story is perfect; every story contains some flaw or an element that some may deem shameful. My hope is that, in my transparency, I can be vulnerable with you and encourage you in turn to be vulnerable with yourself—normalizing the simple fact that we as women, as mothers, and as humans are allowed to fuck up, experience it, learn from it, grow from it, and share it so that we all can find normalcy in being both mothers and also humans.

After I became pregnant, I stalled for weeks, ignoring my sore double-A breasts as they got tender and grew into a B cup before I finally broke down, reluctantly bought a pregnancy test, and watched those two pink lines magically appear on the white stick from the dollar store. As the pink lines became solid, bold, and undeniable, I wailed in fear, as if someone had pitched a knife into my back. I was scared AF, and my FBD looked at me with nothing but disgust at my reaction. I already knew in my gut that I was pregnant, even though I thought ignoring it and praying about it would somehow bring my period on. Suddenly everything blew up in flames, without even the slight courtesy of a two-week notice that my life as I knew it would be ending.

It's human nature and common sense to check in with the person who conspired in your pregnancy when you become pregnant, because without a doubt parenthood is a job for two (or more) people. All children are a gift to the world; however, I think it's important to acknowledge that all circumstances are not. Trying to save a relationship or a person with another person is not a solution. In fact, it is a sure way to fail yourself, the person you're attempting to save, and the small person who didn't ask for any of this shit. Many women resort to what they think they "should" do, which just translates to what society has told us we are obligated to do.

The imaginary checklist I created and checked off really had nothing to do with me or how what I was deciding to embark on was going to affect me. It did, however, have everything to do with what I thought people expected me to do. Overall, the deciding factor for me was a mystic sign from the universe that may sound even crazier than the imaginary list I made up in my head. Within the first four weeks of discovering I was pregnant, naturally, I had an unsettling desire to learn how I should handle this pregnancy. I felt I wasn't equipped for a definite answer on the direction my life should take next. I began reaching out to my witchy friends and the little spiritual community I knew in LA. I prayed on it, repeatedly asking Spirit to deliver me some magical message or sign.

One day, after weeks of asking around, feeling anxious AF, stressing, not knowing what my destiny entailed, I met up with some friends at a gathering in Studio City. We swam all day while people went in and out of this house for hours. At the end of the day, I happened to reach out, mentioning to the group of people closest to me my desperate need to talk to some sort of "spiritual adviser." Sure enough, ask and you shall receive. Spirit must have moved me to ask the host in that very moment. Perplexed by my random question in the middle of a pool day, she responded, "Like a psychic?"

Relieved, I answered, "Yeah, that will do."

"My girlfriend Eddi is here visiting from Australia. She's the best psychic I know, and she's been here all day hanging out in the house."

At that moment, I knew Spirit had heard my cries for help—and whatever answers I received that day, I would accept as a direct answer from her.

A few hours later, our host told me Eddi was ready and waiting inside for me. My heart pounding and stomach turning, I felt as though I was walking to meet my destiny. When I entered the room, I was met with a small-framed white woman with brown, shoulder-length hair; oddly enough, I hadn't yet seen her at the gathering at all. She spoke with an Australian accent, and honestly, she looked more like a preschool teacher than a witch, but hey! Spirit comes in all forms. She shuffled tarot cards in an office that had been transformed into a Zen den for my future. My body and palms became sweaty as I watched the candles flicker. I made a covenant with myself that whatever answers I got in the next few moments were going to reveal to me whether I should keep the baby growing inside of me. As she shuffled, she never asked me what I was dealing with or what I was so desperately seeking on a summer day at a pool party in LA, but somehow the first words she spoke while she shuffled were these: "It seems like whatever's on your heart is a choice that's time-sensitive and needs to be decided on quickly."

This was a fucking understatement if I had ever heard one. The flow of the crimson way had come the first month I was pregnant; the second month seemed to consist of me being frightened as fuck and confused; and approaching month three, here I was at a friend of a friend's house seeking prenatal advice from a stranger-psychic at a pool party—so LA. She continued to shuffle the deck in deep concentration, then began laying the cards down.

I watched her place each card in a cross formation facing up, and as she turned over the third card, I had to squint and shift my body forward to make sure I was certain of what I was seeing. There was a card with what appeared to be a pregnant woman on it. I was so fucking stunned I had to confirm that what I was seeing was right.

Me (*pointing*): "Is that a pregnant woman?"

Eddi: "Yes."

Apparently, Spirit wanted the sign to be crystal fucking clear, because I hadn't even known such a tarot card existed. The message from God I so desperately asked for left little room for dispute. In that single moment, I made the executive decision to go forward with my pregnancy. For me, asking for a sign and then receiving it in such a crystal-clear form was the universe signing, sealing, and delivering the answer to my prayer. I was to become a mother.

The rest of the reading was kind of a blur, but I do remember Eddi mentioning that my baby daddy would step up. Boy, was she wrong about that. I knew that a lot of my friends and some of my family would probably not support my decision; nonetheless, it seemed God had had the last word.

The moral of the story is this: make your own decisions about your body and your life in the way that best fits you—whether it be a personal checklist of pros and cons, a tarot reading by a random psychic lady at a pool party, or an honest conversation with yourself. The truth is that we never really know how our deck will be dealt. As much as we would like to perfectly curate our lives, things rarely work out the way we plan.

For me, seeking answers in mystic form was totally normal and the way I liked to communicate with Source, my ancestors, and my angels. I had always given space for Spirit to stay in contact with me in ways I could recognize in this dimension. When I was a kid, I'd ask God questions, and then the first billboard or street sign I saw that had "Y" in it, for yes, or "N," for no, were my answers. I vividly remember testing my ability to get in touch with Spirit. Even though it sounds crazy, I can honestly say that in adulthood, my ability to stay in tune with that childlike intuition, even through unexpected mediums, has served me. I believe almost anything can be a sign. If you're making a wish at 11:11 and simultaneously a glass breaks unexpectedly, or you're thinking of someone you haven't seen and they call you, it's Spirit affirming your thoughts and reminding you of your powers.

Everyone talks about how great pregnancy is; we've all seen the images of women glowing and grinning and fitting perfectly into their cute and stylish maternity clothes. And don't get me wrong, pregnancy is pretty much great; everyone is extra nice to you, pulling out chairs, opening doors, and fetching snacks because, well, you're growing a damn baby! But no one really shares the unpretty parts of the ten-month bid of pregnancy (yes, ten months!), which is a crash course in taking care of two and sometimes three times as many people (because, yes, your partner is one of them) as you have taken care of for your entire previous life. The truth is there's no amount of time that can realistically prep you for the transition that takes place in the mind, body, and spirit of a pregnant woman. But I couldn't really focus on this transition; I was primarily focused on the ways I could help my BD evolve. He was still heavily dependent on his family for financial and personal support. I started to become resentful because I never had as much support, and I also became annoyed with his family because their support was severely stunting his growth and my plans to make a man out of him.

When I finally came to terms with accepting this life-changing choice, I remember the secret dialogue I had with myself: "If I have to raise this baby alone, I am okay with that." Reflecting on it now, I was convincing myself more than I was believing that statement. I never really admitted out loud to anyone else that I had doubts. I couldn't bring myself to admit that deep down in my heart, I wasn't 100 percent sure that BD and I could "make it" as a family unit, despite my heartfelt desires. I knew my friends and family were having doubts, because they didn't hesitate to point out the obvious issues in our relationship—the ones I had shared with them time and time again and the shit they had witnessed firsthand. I remember calling up my best friend, who was already a single mom of three, and telling her a story about how my BD insinuated I was a ho after a night out with some friends. Her response was brutal but true.

"You know that's how he really feels about you, and it's not going to stop just because you have a baby. You have to decide if that's something you can handle and want to bring a baby into."

She was right. I had become somewhat numb to his harsh words and made excuses for him. As much as I wanted to romanticize my situation, I could see that my BD loved me more than anyone else had ever loved me but also hated parts of me—the parts that longed to be free, independent, and social. I thought, *Maybe now that I'm on my way to being a mother, those parts of me will diminish, and I can change.* Boy, was I wrong. I wish I knew then that if someone loves you, they will love the whole you. Shame will have you hating parts of you that you should really be learning to love.

As time progressed, my body began to morph, and our day-to-day routine took a one-hundred-and-eighty-degree turn. The simple pleasures like going up stairs or walking short distances became difficult. Most women think about the weight they may gain in pregnancy as soon as they learn they're knocked up. I, however, had been under one hundred pounds most of my adult life, with the exception of my freshman fifteen. In fact, my lifelong dream was to gain weight, but when my belly began to come in, and not my ass and thighs, I was pissed, and the rapid weight gain in only my belly still felt foreign AF. Up until my fifth month of pregnancy, I just looked like I drank too many beers, and it wasn't cute.

I couldn't complain, because then every woman would say I was a spoiled skinny bitch, but the truth is no matter what weight you start at, your pregnant body is bound to change in ways you hadn't thought about. There's no way to predict exactly how your body will change, and there's really no way to prepare for such a fast and "alienlike" transition. I refused to buy maternity clothes because I wasn't going to be pregnant very long, and I just kept squeezing into the shit I already had. Even that came with commentary from the peanut gallery: "You're pregnant now. You shouldn't wear that." "You know you're about to be someone's mother. Is that appropriate?" Already people had expectations for me, and as confusing as these were, I'm a stubborn little bitch, and people's comments only made me lean harder into my tiny belly shirts and tight dresses. When my belly finally took form and looked like a pregnant belly, I wouldn't put it away. Pregnancy and motherhood were not about to change Jamilah Mapp.

CHAPTER 3

FUCK,
I Just Had a Baby

The act of giving birth is scary, empowering, and inevitable if you are blessed with a normal pregnancy. Creating a birth plan, educating yourself on real choices, and trusting whatever your body has in store is your first major lesson. Your birth plan, much like life itself, is subject to change. Feeling empowered to advocate for yourself and the woman you used to be is so very important.

ERICA

"They are so easy, and I'm one of few doctors who know how to leave minimal scarring."

My ob-gyn mentioned her expertise in cesarean sections at an early monthly checkup. I listened with deaf, naive ears because I *knew* that I would be having a natural birth. It wasn't the first time she had brought up cesareans, but I figured she was just letting me know my options. Either way, it was a drug-free birth for me. I had been practicing holding ice in the palms of my hands for weeks and mentally preparing for the pain with lots of deep breathing. Dr. C-section had already scared me away from a home birth, and I wasn't going to let a trickle of doubt sneak into my head about my capability to have the experience I wanted. I was delivering at the hospital, with zero intervention, and that was that. So I thought.

My daughter had been kicking me like a professional soccer player for months, and I just knew she was ready to make her debut with no hesitation. As I neared my due date, I became more and more anxious to get her out. My back ached, and if one more person asked me whether I was having twins, I was going to lose it. My mom had heard of a restaurant in LA whose owners swore they had a salad that induced labor. It was called "THE" salad, and it tasted delicious, but it didn't do shit. Nothing was going to rush this stubborn Taurus out of her rent-free home. I drank raspberry-leaf tea and got acupuncture, and still—nothing. Dr. C-section said that my daughter was getting very big and that if my water didn't break by the magical date she predicted, I would need to be induced. I had heard about the negative side effects of Pitocin, a natural hormone that causes the uterus to contract. Pitocin is used to induce labor, strengthen labor contractions during childbirth, control bleeding after childbirth, or induce an abortion. All of which added up, for me, to a big fucking no.

I knew in my heart of hearts that we wouldn't be going down that road. I had not written out my birth plan because I didn't know I needed one. I am certain that if I had had a doula, I would have been more prepared to advocate for myself, but I was made to feel that I didn't need to write a silly list of exactly what I wanted in every scenario. Besides, Dr. C-section was my doula and would never steer me wrong, right? "Doctor knows best" is how I was brought up, and I nervously believed in her. I put the idea of inducement out of my head and focused on the last few things that had to happen before my baby's birth: the baby shower and assembling this 686,238,729-piece crib. My mother planned a beautiful baby shower in LA, and we invited everyone we loved. I hadn't told anyone, besides Mom, what I was going to name my daughter, and we were going to announce the name at the shower.

Side note: Everyone and their mama will have an opinion about your child's name. My tip to you is to not share it. Name your child what speaks to you without intervention and opinion.

BD was so excited and grinning from ear to ear all day. We were so close to the finish line, and it was time to party, something we hadn't done in a very long time. This was the ultimate celebration. I mingled with my guests and saw the gifts stack up on the table. The amount of shit they tell you that you need for one human is insane, and you know I added every last thing to my registry. It was a full house, and we played the baby shower games that everyone tells you to play, including a game of Scrabble in which we revealed our baby girl's name: Irie Jane. She was conceived on our little Jamaican break-up-to-make-up trip, and "Irie" was a Jamaican term that meant good vibes. BD and I smiled with tears in our eyes because it all felt so real. Irie was ours, and we were her cool-ass parents.

As the crowd settled, it was time for a toast. My mom and dad kicked it off, and last but not least, BD got his turn. He toasted my family for their support, and then he toasted me and shared how much he loved me. Then he did something I was not expecting. I mean we had casually joked and teased about it, but I wasn't anticipating it actually happening. As I listened to him share his love for our bond and little family, I barely noticed his friend nervously searching through a backpack behind us. He quickly passed something to my beautiful man, and BD got down on one knee and pulled out a big, beautiful diamond ring.

"Will you marry me?"

I was in shock, but there was no hesitation. I nodded my head because words were too much. Marriage was something I didn't think I wanted, and neither were kids, but here I was, blissfully in love, saying yes to all my nos. I wasn't going to be a statistic. I was showing my family that we were going to get it right. No single mother over here. Nope! I was a whole fiancée now, and the only thing left to do was deliver this baby.

A week before my due date, we set inducement for April 24, 2015. Dr. C-section said it was better to set a date to make sure a hospital bed would be ready for me. She told me that waiting any longer than seven days after my due date would make the probability of a natural birth much lower. Fearmongering was her specialty, and I felt myself falling into her trap.

I went home that day and had a little talk with baby girl in her new room. Over the past few months, I had meticulously prepared her space, and the final touch was the rocking chair where I spent many days deciding what she would look like. My mom had told me that she did the same with me, and I came out looking exactly as she had manifested. Big, curly hair, her daddy's eyes, chocolate skin, dimples, and my lips were what I imagined for Irie Jane. But this time, as I rocked back and forth, I visualized my water breaking in the shower, me giving birth quickly, and BD catching our baby.

As I envisioned what I wanted, I felt overwhelmed with panic. Could I do this? I had spent so much time preparing everything else that I hadn't really thought about the details of my birth. Oh my God, this baby has to get out of me somehow, right? Will she break my pussy? What if I can't push her out? Will they have to use that suction thingy that makes newborn baby heads look like coneheads? What if she suddenly goes breach? Could I die during childbirth? Could she? At the time I had no idea that Black women are three times more likely to die during childbirth than white women, and thank God I didn't, because I would have spiraled even more. My thoughts started to go dark, and so I just stopped thinking about the birth and hoped for the best.

The well-informed woman I am today wishes I could offer that previous version of myself a hug and tell her to keep going, to keep envisioning what she wanted. I wish I could tell her that manifesting and believing in her capabilities would be her superpower and that she could do this exactly the way she wanted. Back then, I called BD 911 and told him to come home immediately and fuck me. Sex is supposed to help induce labor;

he had gotten me into this mess, and he was going to get me out of it. We'd probably had sex six times over the past four months, and even those times were only because I felt bad that my sex drive was at zero capacity. He came home, we did the deed, and still nothing happened.

My due date came and went, and I reluctantly packed my bags and headed to the hospital. We checked into our room, and a wave of fear and doom came over me. I had only ever been in the hospital rooms of sick people. My beloved grandfather had passed away two months before, and all I could imagine was watching his spirit leave his body. The thought that kept ringing through my head was that the hospital was where people came to die. I sat in the uncomfortable bed where I was expected to deliver life and started bawling.

Listen, I've always been a bit dramatic, and for those who happily made that inducement appointment and rolled in like a breeze, I commend you. This was just not what my spirit wanted, and when you go against yourself, your body and mind react in different ways. Mine reacted in dark thoughts, fear, and anxiety. My mom comforted me and helped calm my nerves, and eventually I settled down. Dr. C-section came into the room happy and ready to affirm that I had made the right choice by scheduling life's natural progression. She took my vitals and then checked my cervix. I wasn't dilated. Shocker. Next came that devil bitch named Pitocin, and everything gets a little blurry after that. Knots in my stomach made me feel as though I had taken the strongest laxative of all time and my stomach was having a knife war that I wasn't going to win. I went to the bathroom and sat on the toilet five or six times until my mom finally said to me, "Honey, you don't have to poop. Those are contractions."

"Oh."

BD got me out of bed, and we began to walk the hallways of the hospital. The pain increased with every step I took. All that holding on to ice and Lamaze training wasn't helping shit. We came back to our room, and I tried to get the pain under control. I was failing. I thought the contractions would start off slow, but these were level 10 off the bat. We called in the doctor, and she checked my cervix. I wasn't anywhere near having a baby. She pressed her fingers inside me hard and, boom, my water broke. I wasn't given any notice that this was about to happen. Looking back, I realize the negligence of this act, especially since I had no information about what typically happens after that occurs. Had I known that I had twenty-four hours to get my baby out due to increased risk of infection after a mother's water breaks, I would have asked the doctor to chill on the fingering. Again, not having someone to advocate for me and having no birth plan really left me at the will of others. I continued for the next hour to breathe through these Pitocin-induced contractions, but I gave up and did what I hoped I wouldn't have to: consent to an epidural.

My doctor walked in with someone I assumed was the epidural "expert," and they both explained what they would be doing: plunging a long-ass needle into my spine.

"Just do it now."

I could barely catch my breath, and I just needed the pain to stop. I felt a poke, but the pain was still level 10. Then I felt another poke.

"What is going on?!"

"Sorry, I missed it. I have to do it again."

Another poke. Still no relief.

"What the fuck are you doing?"

Yes, I was raging. I don't talk to people this way, but I had no fucks to give, and the pain of my contractions paired with this unnecessary poking was too much to handle.

Then my doctor said something that took me dissecting Black birth and my birth experience over the past few years to finally acknowledge—that she didn't really protect and care for me.

"He is in training and has administered countless . . ."

"He's *in training?*"

I could not believe that I was being practiced on and was being told only after the fact. Black people have been used for science experiments since the inception of this country, so call it ancestral trauma or just plain negligence, but I was pissed. Once everyone felt my rage, the dose was administered by someone else, and finally . . . sweet relief set in. Epidurals really are magic and probably one of my top five favorite drugs, right up there with MDMA.

The beauty of birthing at Cedars-Sinai in 2015 is that they had no cap on the number of people who can come visit you. It seemed that Irie was going to take her time, so I invited all twenty-five of my friends and family over to watch a very important moment in televised history: Diane Sawyer's interview with Caitlyn (formerly Bruce) Jenner, soon after she came out. Yes, that is what I wanted to watch as I painlessly labored, because it was entertaining and distracted me from the fear of giving birth. At the end of the evening, everyone began to leave, and my doctor checked one last time to see whether I was dilated. Nope, I was still only at 3.5 centimeters, and so we called it a night and went to sleep. When I woke up, I just knew I had to be ready to go. They had been checking me all night, but nothing seemed to progress. Over the next few hours, I started getting the chills. I had a fever, which happens when your water has been broken for an extended amount of time, leaving you susceptible to infection. I was given some meds to bring my fever down, but they only worked temporarily. I was getting nervous: Was my baby in danger? Nurses were shuffling around and not really saying much as I tried to stay calm. Next thing I knew, Dr. C-section was in my face telling me that my baby was under duress and that I had to undergo an emergency—you guessed it—C-section. All her manifestations were coming true, and my worst nightmare had become my reality. BD calmed my nerves with his silliness. One thing I could always count on was him making me laugh. He put on his scrubs and his big goofy smile and talked me down. I realize now that this was my intro to motherhood and life: everything is subject to change.

It wasn't pain—just extreme pressure, as if a baby grand piano was lying on top of me. That's what having my C-section felt like. A lot of it was a blur, but I remember them playing Michael Jackson's "P.Y.T." in the background and BD screaming at the top of his lungs when I felt a jolt in my body. It was my child leaving my womb, and I felt her departure on a spiritual level. My baby was no longer part of me, and I felt her absence. That's the only way I can describe it. I got scared—and her father was screaming so loud I thought something was wrong. Guess we're both dramatic. I remember that it felt as though everyone had left me. I could hear people on the other side of the room talking and I called out for them, but "P.Y.T." was loud and my guts were on the table, making it pretty impossible to make more than a whisper with my lips. Next thing I know, they plopped my baby on my face and told me to smile for a picture. That picture still makes me chuckle. I look high and happy. I was. She was here. My fiancé and the love of my life and I had created life, and she was the most beautiful thing I had ever seen. That sounds corny, but I swear she was fucking perfect.

The next few days at the hospital were exhausting. I swear they intentionally wake up new moms and bother us endlessly to prepare us for the shock we will encounter when we get back home and realize we won't be sleeping for the next nineteen months. I couldn't wait to get out and go home with my family. *My family.* I had created a family—we had. But let's be honest, women, we really run this shit. We make the population, create the village. Future leaders and baby psychopaths—we make them all! We are superior beings. Yes, he did his part, but I did *the* part. These bodies, these beautiful homes that protect, nurture, and birth whole humans out of a vagina—or in my case, my FUPA—are magic and deserve every goddamn flower at the flower shop.

A man does what he can; a woman does what a man cannot.

—ISABEL ALLENDE

Nobody and nothing can prepare you for the level of tiredness you experience in the first few months of having a child. Everyone tells you to sleep when you're pregnant, but you don't listen because you're physically uncomfortable or you don't truly understand the value of rest. Then when you actually have a baby and he or she is asleep, you finally have a second to do X, Y, and Z until the baby wakes up, leaving you exhausted. I am here to scream from the mountaintops: *Go. To. Sleep.* Sleep everywhere and anywhere. Sleep in cars, when your friends come over to help, when the babysitter is over. Go to sleep, girl. Rest becomes a high-value commodity for those first few months. Let people come help you. You don't need to be Superwoman. Ease into your new title, especially if you have the support system to do so. Babies sleep for most of the day the first few months, and so should you. Don't feel bad. You just created life. Go the fuck to sleep.

You know what else they don't tell you? That you may be the one in diapers. I hadn't been out in fourteen days or more, and so Target felt like an easy and safe option for a first day outside. As I got out of my car to go to the store, I realized that my butt was all wet. I looked at the seat and it was soaked. I had peed on myself and hadn't even felt it. Postpartum urinary incontinence is a real thing that nobody had warned me about. I cried as baby daddy went up to Target to buy me adult diapers.

What was happening to my body? Was it ever going to be mine again?

On top of all this, my body dysmorphia began to creep back. I had had my child but still looked somewhat pregnant, and that seventy pounds I had gained really showed now. I looked in the mirror and could think only about all the diets I needed to start. I didn't look like the cute skinny Instagram moms who seemed to look perfect one month after giving birth (hello, Jamilah!). Everything was big, including these DDD breasts my daughter had gifted me. I sat and tried not to smother her with them as I breastfed her. I had been robbed of my natural birth experience, but I knew that at the very least I would get to experience the next most natural thing a mother can do for her child: feed her with this liquid gold milk flowing from this new favorite part of my body. Yes, I didn't love peeing on myself, the nasty scar, or the spongy, rolly stomach I had acquired, but these boobs were a gift from the pregnancy gods. I just knew that they were ready to feed this beautiful little human with ease.

Wrong. Irie had a hard time latching on, and after weeks of trying, successfully and unsuccessfully, my nipples were hanging on by a thread. Nipple covers were the only way I could breastfeed her, and my milk supply began to drop. I felt ashamed. How could I not produce enough milk for my daughter? Her pediatrician suggested that I supplement with formula before ever suggesting a lactation specialist. Everyone around me, including friends and family, were constantly telling me that my baby was hungry every time she cried, which further deepened my anxiety around feeding time. I gave in and started giving her formula around three months. I was exhausted; I felt I had tried everything I could to be her only food source. I did try, with the limited information I was given, but even today I still have some shame around not sticking it out or trying harder. There are so many resources for women who struggle with breastfeeding. Also, sometimes you just can't do it, and that is okay.

This all sounds terrible, and to be honest, the first few months after having a baby are kind of terrible. Birthing a human is an exciting, life-altering experience that you must give yourself time to adjust to. Your body will heal, you'll drop those pounds, and you'll get the hang of it all, but it's a process that takes time. Being kind to yourself is the first and most important lesson. Your child feels everything. Babies are new, sensitive souls, and their mamas are their entire universe. Oftentimes, dads don't know where to fit in at the beginning, but they will find their groove if you let them. Irie's dad happily took on his new role, and his years of insomnia finally came to good use during middle-of-the night feedings and crying sessions. We were a team, and even though everything didn't go as planned, I was happy to have a healthy, beautiful baby and a partner who loved us both. As I held Irie in my arms while he slept next to me, I thought, *This was meant to be, and this is how it will be forever.*

MILAH

I had very little experience in birth, but in high school I knew a girl who got knocked up early while attending our Catholic school and had little support, so I volunteered to accompany her to the hospital. Long story short, she ended up having to be rushed to the OR for a cesarean, and I vividly remember that everything leading up to that point seemed pretty fucking terrifying. I watched nurses scurry around her and machines beep and screech without a single nurse or doctor saying a single word to my scared teenage friend, who was actually birthing. It wasn't even me lying helpless on that electric bed, but the experience scarred me for life.

Years later, when I went off to college to have the Black experience I had been deprived of growing up, I met a bunch of hippie Black people unlike anybody I had ever encountered in the very sheltered, very Caucasian suburbs of San Fernando Valley where my family lived. These people were Afrocentric, and they grew their own food and weed and birthed their own babies, free of doctors and hospitals. As soon as I heard the stories of women being surrounded by friends and family in the comfort of their own homes, my intuition knew that was the real way women were meant to bring life into the world. You see, when you're a woman it's important to tap into what resonates with your spirit. We are often so conditioned to give our power away and ask for outside input, when we already have the answers seeded deep inside of ourselves. Just because someone has credentials doesn't necessarily mean that person has all the right answers for you.

I was determined that I would have this kind of birth—but I was young and broke, and I didn't have the five thousand dollars for a midwife. So I studied every home-birth video the academy of YouTube had to offer, OD'd on every orgasmic birth podcast and every hypno-birth article, and read every book Ina May Gaskin ever wrote (highly recommended). I prepped my partner in every possible way, ordered a kiddie pool and a full birth kit, and decided I'd rather have an unassisted home birth than a hospital one. Extreme, I know.

However, the number one lesson in motherhood came crashing

down around me, reminding me that I, in fact, was not always in control and that I would have to submit to life's flow if I wanted to remain in peace. My home-birthing dreams were thwarted when my blood pressure spiked at thirty-seven weeks, forcing me to be hospitalized and induced. I'll never forget the disappointment I felt when my doctor told me at my weekly visit that I should check myself into labor and delivery. The delivery ward was a place I had been avoiding for the past eight months. My doctor insisted I just "check it out" and take the tour, "in case I ended up there." In that moment, I felt she was against me, along with every other medical professional who had been brainwashed by their $300,000 degrees and Western medicine textbooks.

Even though Erica and I hadn't met at this point, I had also watched Ricki Lake's award-winning film *The Business of Being Born*, just as Erica did while pregnant. I knew that once I entered those hospital doors, there were bound to be "up sales" and interventions that would interfere with what my body was naturally built to do. In my months of research, I had gained an immense amount of respect and trust in my body and my ability to tap into this primitive part of me that inherently I was fully equipped with. Unbeknownst to me, all my research had given me faith in my body and my feminine power. I was becoming aware that I was the sacred portal of life, the closest thing that humanity would come to the creator, and no Western standards of medicine could trump that power. I wasn't sick, and hospitals were for sick people, right?

I continued smoking cannabis throughout my pregnancy; my BD was aware and okay with me smoking, and so was I. Instinctively I knew that the plant medicine wasn't going to harm me or my child, and I stuck to my decision. I tried to do some research, but there are few to no accurate studies online. I thought about the women in Jamaica, who surely consumed the holy plant during pregnancy, and I talked to other mamas who smoked cannabis during their pregnancies without any complications. I smoked privately at night in the comfort of my own home and surprisingly got very little shit from the people in my life. My mom talked shit, but that was a given, and I didn't care.

I learned early on that the less people knew, the less ammo they had to bitch about, a prime lesson in motherhood that will get you far.

Moms often write in and ask about our experience with cannabis in pregnancy and with breastfeeding; many of them are suffering from morning sickness, depression, anxiety, or something else that cannabis can be helpful for. Most of these mothers consumed before they were pregnant, but they suddenly feel pressure to stop and often feel shame and guilt about having the desire to smoke or the need. Let me be clear: I'm no medical expert. But if doctors can green-light a long list of hard-core pharmaceuticals during pregnancy, then the natural plant created by God can surely be included on that list. I personally have more faith in the medicines provided for us by Mother Nature. I urge everyone to do what sits right with their spirit. I'm learning that in womanhood and in motherhood, our intuition always has the answers. I continued to smoke cannabis during pregnancy and breastfeeding, and I was able to do it in peace. If paranoia, guilt, and shame are bound to show up for you, then don't partake. Just know it's your choice, your baby, and your body. Whatever choice you make, be at peace with it, and trust yourself— another prime lesson in motherhood.

Over the months, I'd felt comfortable being honest with my ob-gyn about my reservations with Western medicine and didn't hesitate to let her know I had done my research. She was aware of my birth plan.

"Your blood pressure is really high. I think you need to go check into the delivery ward now," she said.

I thought to myself, *WTF is she talking about?* We had just gone through an entire routine appointment during which everything looked fine.

Now I was laughing. "What do you mean, *now*? I was about to get up and leave. If the nurse hadn't said anything to you, I would have been on my way home."

"No, Jamilah, I would have reviewed the chart after the appointment and called you to come back."

"Can't I just go home and see if it goes down? How much of an emergency is high blood pressure exactly? Because I feel fine!"

As much as I had consumed natural hippie pregnancy shit, I was still scared when she told me I had to be checked into the hospital that evening, three weeks before I was due. I wanted to just go home, crawl into a ball, cry, and try to have sex so the baby would come down naturally. Instead, my baby daddy's sister took me to Panda Express, where I attempted to eat orange chicken while I decided what I wanted to do (a.k.a. come to the same decision as the doctor but on my own terms). I called a few people to get some advice, but ultimately nobody, not even myself, could ignore my doctor's urge for me to check myself into the maternity ward.

Defeated, I went back to the hospital, checked in, undressed, got hooked up to the monitors and that awful IV, got some sort of generic testosterone inserted in my pussy to help induce my labor, and waited in complete and utter fear. Rightfully so, because not even an hour later, my contractions began to kick in like the motherfuckin' Karate Kid. For the next forty-eight hours, I struggled with agonizing pain. Hearing a bunch of women screaming down the halls throughout the delivery ward didn't help. During my stay, at least ten of my friends and family members came in and out of my hospital room, including my dad, who thought it was a great idea to crack jokes, drink bottles of beer, and FaceTime extended family while I cursed him out and laughed between contractions. I placed affirmations all over the walls, bounced on that big-ass labor ball thing that everybody recommends, danced, walked around the hospital, showered, and even tried to hit a joint in the parking lot, IV in tow. I forced the nurses to print out and make copies of my very specific handwritten birth plan that I had made just in case of a hospital emergency. I was a hot and stubborn mess. I absolutely refused to get the epidural, because that was not included in my pregnancy plan. I recall the contractions creeping up my spine seemingly every five minutes, increasing in pain like roaring waves swelling, then crashing, over and over and over again. At one point I remember looking around the room at my friends, family, and baby daddy all sleeping and telling myself, *Be quiet. Nobody here can help you anyway.*

Birth forces you to go inside of your soul, open up doors, and discover new hallways and rooms inside yourself that you never knew were there.

After two nights of suffering, having my water break, accepting a drowsiness-inducing drug that my birth plan specifically requested that I not be offered, and then having some sort of weird, water-filled balloon inserted in my pussy, I had opened up only four fucking centimeters. I knew it wouldn't be long before they would discover some sort of infection or emergency, so I accepted an epidural, because, honestly, my body had endured enough. It felt as though I had given up on everything I had said I wanted, but sometimes the lesson is detachment from the plan.

I took that epidural and went from the exorcist to an angel. I can now proudly say epidurals are the shit, and I was tripping not to accept it sooner. I napped, woke up nine centimeters dilated, secretly had my baby daddy get me a Red Bull (because the hospital denies women food or drinks during labor), asked everyone to leave the room so I could down it, and then I was ready to rock and roll. I gave myself a pep talk, texted all my friends around 5:03 p.m. that I was about to push, and by 5:12 p.m. I attentively watched in the mirror I requested—because when else could I witness my body do some shit like this?—as Luna's head and little body slithered out of my yoni like a little alien out of a can. I was in utter shock and amazement. The very moment I felt Luna's warm little body hit my chest, something cosmic took place. My soul was reuniting with someone it had missed very much and had known a million times before. I knew I had unlocked something buried deep down inside of me.

For me, birth was a rite of passage and a journey to depths of my being that I never knew existed.

The days after Luna's birth were by far the happiest days of my life. After years of fantasizing and pulling out, my little family was complete. When I looked at my BD hold our daughter, I was overwhelmed with happiness. I was in pure bliss. I had a baby with my best friend of more than thirteen years; we weren't perfect, but we had an apartment, a little old car, and each other and that felt like more than I could ever ask for. Every time I laid eyes on this precious baby, my eyes swelled with tears and my heart overflowed with pure happiness. I'll never forget getting to our apartment for the first time with Luna in tow. After seventy-two hours of around-the-clock care, it dawned on me that I was alone with this tiny, fragile, living, breathing human.

Still, as happy as I was, something was off. I had spent nine months pregnant, only to be transformed into a standing milk cow. My belly was ten shades darker than the rest of my body, as were my ginormous *National Geographic* nipples, and every time I coughed, laughed, or peed, my vagina hurt, even though I was barely torn. Was I ever going to feel or look the same again? I had been poked, pushed, and pinned at the hospital, and my body was starting to feel like a machine. A few days after I came home, I experienced some slight headaches and was encouraged to go back to the hospital by my ob-gyn. I had to wait in the ER for hours before anyone would listen to me, only to be told by a physician's assistant that I needed a CAT scan (I did not). I was only five days into motherhood, and I was breaking down. Finally, after I had repeated my story ten times to ten separate medical professionals in urgent care, my doctor came and advocated for me to be checked into the maternity ward, where I should have been moved hours earlier for postpartum high blood pressure.

I was ignorant then about racism in medical care; looking back, I see that this postpartum experience was trash and likely racist. Eventually, I was hooked up to a magnesium IV for twenty-four straight hours, which gave me a migraine way worse than the one I came in with. Apparently, it was supposed to reduce my blood pressure. For the first few hours I was there, I was accompanied by my BD and newborn, until they were asked to leave for liability reasons. I was pissed! After I had spent twenty-four straight hours babyless in the maternity ward, my BD returned to get me, and all the nurses swooned over how amazing he was for being able to keep his newborn for twenty-four fuckin' hours. I was perplexed. It was my first glimpse of how dads get glorified for doing their job. Finally, after this ordeal, I got to go home.

About two weeks into motherhood, my baby daddy asked me for some head, and I almost lost my shit. Was this what I had signed up to do for the rest of my life? Supply others with . . . me? I was pissed, and suddenly all the hype of "wife life" felt more like *The Twilight Zone*. The word "forever" began to ring and really sink in, like a horror film I couldn't escape. Couldn't this muthafucker see how much I had just given? How my body and spirit had just experienced something out of this fucking world?

At that moment, I felt postpartum depression creeping in my back door. I tried to fight it by jumping headfirst back into my life. I literally took Luna to the mall at seven days old, and a random stranger looked over at me and said, "That newborn needs to be inside." I was mad and ignored the fuck out of that woman. Who was this stranger, and was I already a terrible mother? I went back to work with Luna two weeks after giving birth. I even made it to a New Year's Eve party four weeks postpartum, again with Luna in tow and all of us in matching tuxedo outfits. I was determined to preserve some of my old life, and honestly, my baby daddy mostly supported me in that, as long as he was included in all my activities. Soon, though, returning to work, which I'd done to regain some sense of normalcy, just stressed me out more. Taking care of a tiny human and a household and struggling to reevaluate who I was at this stage of my life really put emphasis on what wasn't being done around my house and the support I wasn't getting from my partner. I needed stability more than ever, because "I" was now "we." Worrying about another person's well-being is one thing, but when another life is depending on you, shit shifts.

Bottom line: if you're reading this and you're pregnant, I have three pieces of advice. Do your research, insist your partner also do their research, and together envision your perfect birth (because orgasmic birth does exist—look it up), but expect the unexpected. Understand that what your body is about to experience is as close as your physical body will ever get to God; it's powerful and deeply spiritual. Know that things are inevitably about to change, but remember, in the words of the best advice on motherhood I ever received, "The baby is coming into your life and not the other way around." So often we see new mothers make accommodations without considering what also works for them. They abandon the lifestyle they had before the baby was born, when it's actually okay to integrate your baby into your world. Sometimes the key to "bouncing back" is literally just doing it. Go to the mall or the New Year's Eve party with your baby in tow. Some may think that those were bad choices, but for me, those were the choices I needed to make to preserve the parts of me that made me "me."

Part 2

AD
(AFTER DADDY)

CHAPTER 4

BREAKING
Point

A truer statement has never been made than this: "You make plans, and God laughs at them." As you journey through life, you start to understand all these old sayings you've heard growing up more and more deeply. That's because history repeats itself, and nobody's story is completely unique. But you know what's rare and even revolutionary? The act of choosing yourself—especially when you're a mother.

ERICA

My life burned down in one day. At least that's what it felt like at the time. I wish I could say I saw it coming, but I didn't. With no opportunity to brace for impact, I was left with a hole in my chest the size of the ocean and a two-year-old toddler with baby daddy's exact face.

I was days away from putting down the deposit on our dream Jamaican wedding and sending out my perfectly curated "bridesmaid" proposals when it happened. Cheating, of course, had been a thing, but we had weathered a shitstorm—an abnormally large shitstorm. I had been a "ride or die" partner. I spent the summer of 2016 traveling back and forth with our toddler to

Affirmation
When bad things happen, I am certain that good things are on the way.

Europe, where baby daddy was wrongfully accused, jailed, and facing ten years in prison. I became a part-time detective and legal expert, fighting to ensure Daddy made it back home to our family even after I discovered he had been cheating on the road again. I drove a wedge in my relationship with my mom, validating him and all his bad choices. I ignored the women and somehow reasoned that it was my karma for being a cheater in my teens and early twenties. I played it cool as I spent many nights and mornings of my pregnancy and early post-pregnancy alone while he worked late in the studio or spent time at the strip club doing "research" for his music. I held him and consoled him as it seemed every best friend of his I had never heard of became a casualty to the streets. Because baby was a thug, and I was the Carmela to his Tony Soprano.

Okay, fine, I'm being extra. But Carmela was the shit, and she held it the fuck down, because that's what we're told to do as "valuable" mothers and women. Stand by your man through thick and thin—and, man, was it thin, especially after I gave birth. I had told myself lies about how happy I was because I needed this to be what I wanted it to be: a success story starring me, him, and Irie Jane. I told myself that everything—the women, his career, and his blatant ignoring of my needs—would settle down eventually, that we were both going through a transition, and that "nothing worth fighting for is easy." That toxic-ass piece of conventional wisdom will have you fucked up out here, ladies.

But when I got a picture in my DMs of a pregnant woman claiming to be the "baby mama" of my soulmate, my best friend, my man? That's when I knew my boundaries and self-respect had reached their limits.

A baby? Was it true?

It was.

How could he? After everything we'd been through; after all the promises we had made to each other; after we had faced prison, death, and so much more together—how?

He denied that he was the father, but I didn't care. My intuition, which I had been ignoring for years, said "Bitch, it's done. Don't be that girl. Run." I couldn't even fathom how I would rationalize staying in this situation to myself or my friends and family. Even if it wasn't true, and this woman was as "crazy" as he claimed, I couldn't continue to raise my daughter in this space of uncertainty, unpredictability, and negativity. I had to have compassion for myself and not just him all the time. So how did I make sure I would hold myself accountable and wouldn't go back to him? I called everyone I loved and told them. I needed to say it out loud. I needed to stop making excuses and holding secrets in my body for him. I knew how crazy it all sounded and that I would be embarrassed if I went back. With every call I made, it became more real: This wasn't a dream, and I was never going to wake up the same again. My relationship was over.

The first few weeks were brutal. Shit, the first few months were. My house was empty—just me and my baby. Emotional warfare had also ensued, with remorse and threats of suicide, triggering my trained response to make sure he was okay. He needed emotional support, and I gave it to him at times, because that's what you do when you love an undiagnosed narcissist. You nurse the wounds they gave you, while also licking theirs. You don't want them to hurt themselves, because you can't imagine living in a world without their chaos. And your child needs them, unhealthy or not.

Now, before all the baby daddies of the world go up in arms about women who've been scorned labeling all men narcissists, I will say that I agree that this is a term that gets thrown around way too loosely. Labeling my child's father this way is not something I take lightly, especially knowing that one day my daughter may read this book. I am speaking as someone who has gone to therapy, done the work, asked the questions, observed behavior past and present, spoken to other people who know this person, questioned whether I was actually the narcissist—only to come back to this descriptive word that just, well, fits him. I'm no doctor, but I've interviewed enough experts to know that loving a narcissist is like slow dancing in a burning house. Everyone sees that you're moments away from catching on fire except you. It feels impossible to get out, and in fact you don't want to, and as the smoke fills your lungs with love and fear, the idea of dying alone together in chaos feels beautifully romantic. You're being love-bombed to death all the while, so you don't even realize you're actually suffocating.

Megan Dorty, a narcissism expert and a friend of our podcast, said in our "How to Spot a Narcissist" episode that dating a narcissist is like "death by a thousand cuts." That was us—a thousand little cuts led me to the final stab in the heart. Now, I'm not claiming to be perfect. I was judgmental, defensive, unmotivated, unsexual, depressed, and passive-aggressive. I admit that. Was I all those things all the time? No. I'm not a monster. But I definitely flowed in and out of all those labels. I am not perfect, and neither is he. I am just a woman who has been in a lot of therapy and can finally see myself and that relationship with a clear heart and mind.

Five or six months after the breakup, I still had deep compassion for him and was enraged at everything this "crazy" woman was doing to our family. I couldn't escape the pain and waves of anger. I got down on my knees and begged God to wake me up from this nightmare. I sent emotional texts in the middle of the night asking him how he could do this to our family. I sent him copies of all the love letters that he had written me in jail and over the span of our seven-year relationship. I stalked the "crazy" woman, compared myself to her, wondered what had made him carry on a relationship with her for months behind my back. We were such different women. I reread the texts she forwarded to me documenting his lies about me and talking shit about my family and friends. He had offered to pay for an abortion. How many other women had he put through this? Was she really "crazy," or did he make her crazy with his false promises, his pressure on her to abort her pregnancy, and the silent treatment? Who was this man I had loved unconditionally for so long? Had he ever even loved me? Did he have the true capacity?

I hollered in bed and cried uncontrollably alone and in the arms of friends. I didn't eat. I overate. Repeat, repeat. I put on a brave face for my sweet toddler, who didn't ask for any of this. I felt it all and broke down the moment she went to sleep or was distracted by *Peppa Pig* in the other room. I needed to unravel, and I did. It was important, even if I didn't know why at the time.

I was about to turn thirty in a few weeks and had previously planned a beautiful trip with him, our daughter, and friends to Belize. I canceled his ticket and brought the nanny instead. I almost didn't go, but the trip was the catalyst I needed to feel like Erica again—or at least the new, brokenish version of Erica. I finally pulled myself together, got my hair done, and bought some new bathing suits to make myself feel better. Somewhere between depression and donuts, I had dropped those last after-baby twenty pounds that I had thought I would never lose. When I touched down in Belize, I felt as though I had escaped reality for a moment. My friends were the dose of happiness I needed—them, and a lot of tequila. My little tribe. I had always had a close group of friends, but they became lifesavers as I evolved as a woman and mother.

Reality set back in after I came home from my trip and quickly realized that Stella hadn't actually gotten her groove back. I mean, grooves were made, but I'm not going to feed you this idea that a vacation or a few nights with the girls is going to pull you out of a tragedy. When the pain is deep, you will have to release it many times, and this shit penetrated my entire being. I couldn't stop hearing those two words ringing in my head over and over again: "single mom."

How would I ever get used to calling myself that? This wasn't the plan. Would people ask me what had happened? Was I less valuable? Could I ever love again? Should I try to make it work? Maybe in a few years?

I was having a conversation with podcast icon Joe Budden

during our episode with him, and he said that for a woman, be-coming a single parent is a choice—that women choose to leave for "self-righteous" reasons such as cheating or lying and then kick and scream about their free will to choose to be a "baby mama" every chance they get. He said that we sign up as the "primary parent" and that we "shouldn't have left" if we didn't want this primary role. He's right—not about most of what he said, but yes, I did choose to leave. I could have stayed. Many women do. But I had reached a breaking point. Staying would have been betraying every cell in my body that shuddered at the thought of intimacy with this person, or forgiving him.

The visuals that played in my head of him with her made me sick. The ways I imagined he called just to tell her she was beau-tiful the way he did for me gutted me. I fought every day to get out of bed and move forward. My greatest fear was being a single mom, but I couldn't change the way I felt even if I had wanted to. The months passed, and the pain increased. Yes, increased. There was a child on the way, and it wasn't mine. My daughter was going to have a sibling forever. So, no. I'm not going to tell you some bullshit like getting over heartbreak is easy. It's not. I had to face that I was now a "baby mama," and not the cute kind you see on Etsy shirts bought by married white women. No, I was a Black single mom whose rapper baby daddy had a baby on her. I mean, could it get any more stereotypical? Damn, Erica.

My fear of staying greatly outweighed my fear of leaving. I had reached my limit. Embarrassment and complete shock trumped my heart's impulse to work it out or blame myself for this major fuckup. My financial stability still relied on him in ways. His guilt and his understanding of his responsibility gave me time to figure out how I would afford this new single life on my own. My family gathered around me, and my friends swooped in and helped however they could.

I still had terrible days when I fantasized about the life we were supposed to have, and raging days when I wrote paragraph-long texts of profanities only to delete them before sending. I couldn't fathom getting to the other side of this betrayal and that "everything happens for a reason." There could be no logical reason that God would get all up in my business and ruin my life so swiftly. But God, Spirit, or whatever you believe in always has a plan. I promise you that. It sounds fucking corny, and I hated hearing it, but it's the truth. If you had told me back then that I'd be writing a book, leading retreats, or sharing all my bad choices on the internet when I was in the thick of pain—or that sharing bits and parts of my story could help other women, who in turn would help heal me—I would not have believed it. No fucking way. Listen, I am not special. I am not unique. I am not different from you. I just finally had had enough, and I chose the unknown because that seemed better than stomaching the piping-hot shit meal I was served.

As we began to disassemble our home life together, it became easier to pull myself out of bed every day. We began to navigate coparenting, and I had more alone time to be with myself, to look in the mirror and say, *Who are you? What excites you? What's next?* I had the time to finally say yes to the many invitations I had been saying no to. When you're wrapped up in your relationship, it's easy to pick Netflix and chill over a night with the girls. It's easy to gloss over the signs that your relationship may not be what you think it is and to confuse red flags with the

Face the Fear

This exercise is for the mamas in unhappy relationships who are contemplating whether or not to leave or stay. Write down a list of reasons you are fearful of being a single parent and a list of reasons you are scared to stay. Compare them. Which is worse?

FEAR OF LEAVING ☐   **FEAR OF STAYING** ☐

When you look at the list you've made, try your hardest to step outside of your pain and fear. I know—how do you do that? It's hard AF, but many of our reasons for staying are based on a fear of losing love and stability. We think that we will somehow be ruining our children, that we won't have a place to live, or that our lifestyle will change. All these things may be true. Some of us, me included, have allowed our partners to be our financial provider. Some of us have become our partner's financial provider. What will he do if I leave? What will I do? He might struggle, and so might you. Your kids may feel uncomfortable for a while. Nobody said change was easy.

Try to look at this list as if your best friend had answered these questions—as if she was battling between staying and leaving. We are often more realistic and harsher when it comes to protecting the people we love than when we are protecting ourselves. If your bestie was struggling in her relationship with an abuser, would you tell her to stay for the kids? I hope not. If you saw your child in a relationship that made her or him mostly sad, would you tell your child to thug it out? I doubt it. Give yourself the same grace you would give your best friend or your child. It's not different. Look at this as an opportunity to reparent yourself and give yourself the gentle or hard-AF shove that you need.

color orange. My normally scheduled programming had been interrupted—and thank God. Because I was boring AF, and that wasn't the Erica I had once known.

It's so important to not isolate yourself from the people who make up parts of the "you" before children. Granted, some of those people may have to go if they no longer serve your higher good, and that includes people who don't support the new you that you are choosing to become. On an episode we did with Sarah Nicole Landry, a.k.a. @thebirdspapaya, she explained that it took her three years to divorce her husband and that it happened on a very uneventful Wednesday. She had made her choice, but the people around her needed answers: someone to blame, something to fix. Not all breakups blow up in your face as mine did. Some burn out slowly. Either way, you don't owe anyone an answer for choosing yourself. If you've chosen to leave, it's usually not hasty. Your friends and family are not there day in and day out, experiencing your reality. They aren't in your body while it's screaming and yelling at you in the form of depression, anxiety, overeating, undereating, overdrinking, and feeling less than excited by the presence of that boner in your back as you pray to God he'll believe you're asleep. Nope. So don't ask for permission. Don't ask for too many opinions. You know the answer; you probably just don't like it.

Now for those of you who are happily partnered or married, congratulations! This chapter may or may not speak to you, but I would like to encourage you to peel back a few more layers. If you've just had a child, much has shifted, and you may be over-due for a quality-of-life check-in. Are you guys prioritizing your joy as a couple, or do you just talk about the baby all day long?

Mothers, we have a way of doing this. I get it. We're high off this new exciting thing in our lives, but give it a rest. It's not sexy. STFU about your kids for a day and do some eye-gazing with your lover. What's that? Well, you essentially sit cross-legged facing each other, hold hands, and stare into each other's eyes for an extended period of time. Sounds strange, because it is, if you're used to doing the same ole shit with your partner. This time is crucial to keep your connection alive. Kids really get in the way of that. They are a beautiful distraction from pouring into you and your relationship cup. Go on dates, buy sex toys, hang out with your friends, do things without each other. For God's sake, keep that connection alive, because I want you guys to be the gold standard in a world where the divorce rate is rising every year and pandemics and social media are making human connection less and less appealing.

I'm not sure whether I'll be single or married by the time this book comes out, but what I do know is that choosing myself during this very pivotal year in my life was the catalyst to choosing myself over and over again after that. It's like drinking wine; the first time may not be so great, but then suddenly you're the wino of the group, helping your friends not choose the cheap shit. Prioritizing yourself is an acquired taste. It's kinda nasty at first, and it's not always popular. But for those of us who do it, we can't stop once we pop. In fact, things really get fun after that.

MILAH

For me, on the other hand, the white-picket-fence fantasy of life with my high school sweetheart suffered a very slow death.

> ## Affirmation
> Advocating for and keeping my peace
> is my birthright, and no one comes before me when it
> comes to my well-being.

I allowed the "me" to slowly drain out of me. The process began with me gaslighting myself: normalizing erratic behavior, confusing being patient with being just dumb. I avoided going out for "me time" simply to prevent arguments. I even began believing that my obsession with his not doing what I thought he should do was an excuse for my not being where I wanted to be. I made excuses for his behavior and excuses for my ignoring the behavior. I pushed down my concerns and ignored my fears that my family goals were not being met. I became so good at not feeling that I started to not feel anything.

I morphed into a master numb-er. I numbed myself out by drowning in the happiness of motherhood. I figured I'd be ungrateful to acknowledge all the things I was unhappy with after being granted this new, healthy baby. So many women wished for a healthy pregnancy and newborn—who was I to complain? It was as if the world told me I should be happy, and so I was. I smiled, I basked in early morning cuddles, new coos, and intimate feedings. Of course, there wasn't room for a multitude of feelings. You can't be in bliss and also be unhappy. How selfish would I be to complain about the small things? I mean, millions of women were experiencing far worse situations than mine. I was healthy, I had a source of income, a place to live, and food on the table, so I was all right—right?

Minimizing my pain was something I had learned in childhood, from my parents; one of their favorite sayings was "Kids in Africa are starving! Be grateful you have a roof over your head and food on the table!" Even though my parents had a valid point, I subconsciously decided that feelings of discomfort I experienced were nothing more than complaints and showed a lack of gratitude for the things that I did have. This childhood lesson that many of us learn is aimed at teaching us gratitude and resilience, but it can also be deeply detrimental to understanding our own feelings as valid, and it can encourage us to dismantle the inner alarm systems that are our intuition. Now I know this attitude to be toxic positivity—programming yourself to be so thoroughly "positive" that you aren't able to distinguish your own happiness from unhappiness. This attitude is one many women fall victim to.

That's the thing about the toxic motherhood image: it doesn't leave space for the humanity part. There's this fucked-up idea that to be a good mom, you have to be a good wife, a great housekeeper, happy at all times—and you end up abandoning all traces of your former self. That former self almost has to die so you can prove that you have transformed yourself into what our media-saturated society insists a mother should be.

There were days I felt like an impostor, a child playing house. It seemed that I was supposed to just give birth, then wake up the next day and be a natural at this new full-time job that came with absolutely no hands-on training. I remember having to go to a doctor's appointment with my newborn, with that big-ass bulky car seat of hers, and my "mother-in-law." The waiting room was full of women, and Luna began to squirm and fuss a bit. As I tried to console her, she began to cry more, and I just remember awkwardly maneuvering her into different positions in an attempt to calm her. Naturally, everyone in the office began to look over at us, and suddenly I felt like every woman in the office was judging me, including my partner's mom. Whether or not this was true, that's how I felt. I began to sweat. Fuck. Wasn't I supposed to know how to do this now? Laying her down in my arms, patting her over my shoulder, bouncing her, rocking her, I was panicking on the inside. So I finally walked with her outside the doctor's office into the hallway, where I could breathe. Eventually, she stopped crying, and I looked her in the face and thought, *How the fuck am I supposed to know what you want when you can't even talk?* What the fuck had I gotten myself into? Moments later, another woman walked past me with the same ginormous car seat, but her baby was huge compared with Luna, who was only days old. At that moment, it dawned on me that my sweet, six-pound, tiny baby was about to grow and evolve, and there wasn't shit I could do but grow, too, and figure it out.

How I felt that day in the doctor's office is the way a lot of women feel in the early to not-so-early stages of motherhood—fucking awkward. To describe this time and space between birth and early motherhood as "transformative" is an understatement. There were constant *Twilight Zone* moments that echoed "forever" and scared the shit out of me. There was no end in sight—not that I wanted an out. But the reality had hit that this was not some "stage" in my life; this was a forever commitment connected to two whole-ass people—a baby who couldn't even verbally tell me what was wrong with her and an adult who somehow had the same problem. I felt stuck between a baby and a hard place—or, in my case, a hard dick. Either way, I was lost.

Thinking about multiplying the amount of energy I was exerting now times five, ten, or possibly even fifteen years scared me enough to eventually shake shit up.

I knew that acknowledging my own voice would shift things for everyone: myself, my partner, his family, my child, and so on. I wasn't sure whether the outcome of the shaking would be good or bad, but I knew the shit had to get shook, because I didn't have the capacity to find out what it would feel like years and years down this dreadful road of settling. Nobody tells us—especially women and mothers—that it's okay to simply grow apart from someone. The "I'm just over this shit" box is a valid selection among life's multiple-choice options and should be honored and selected often. People grow, as plants and trees grow. We change, we morph. People around you will journey and grow at different speeds; it's normal and to be expected.

In addition to adjusting to motherhood, I was also adjusting to understanding the way the world viewed motherhood. Not going to lie—care for mothers felt pretty minimal once I was on the other side of childbirth. I went on a short road trip with my BD and his family, and when we arrived at the hotel late, I was starving and also breastfeeding, which takes starving to a whole other level. As my BD was supposed to go grab me food before the closest restaurant closed, he conveniently caught a cramp at 9:45 p.m. (*insert eye roll here*). What I am about to say next may sound heartless, but I don't care. This grown-ass man doubled over in the fetal position on the hotel floor and whimpered in pain as both of his grown-ass parents hovered over him in concern. Not to say I wasn't concerned, but I was newly postpartum, hungry, tired, and with a newborn, and the three adults I was with didn't seem concerned at all. After my BD drank some water and the ordeal was over, I was offered cold potato wedges, because now everything had closed.

This anecdote may seem unimportant, but for me it was an indication of the family structure I had in a sense "married into" when I had a baby. This idea that my BD should be catered to, while I cared for him and his child, seemed to become more and more of a deeply settled condition of my life.

I had witnessed my BD be dismissive and disrespectful to his mother, who had done everything to help in every aspect of his life—signs I had ignored, just as she did. For women, it has seemed natural to protect, excuse, and pave ways for men who aren't reciprocal. Not just reserved for romantic partnerships, this pattern has existed in every facet of male-female relationships, with women the protectors of fragile egos, compensating for men's erratic behavior. I say this as an observer of and culprit in the systems I've personally enabled. Was this pattern in our nature, or had we been conditioned and reduced to this by the patriarchy we have been born and bred in?

Writing this book, I debated a lot about the weight of my words in the next few chapters and the sting my words may cause my family and my daughter, who will inevitably one day read my writing. Who would I be if, given this platform, I used it to reduce my feelings in order to appease people who conceal their own truths? One thing that building the podcast has taught me is that brutal, raw honesty is necessary and relatable. It's relatable because, no matter who or where we are, we all got some shit. Like the testimonies of religion, "the word" is essential in recruiting believers. But my goal isn't to recruit anyone to believe just as I believe or to convince people to ditch their own belief systems. This "word" is simply to encourage other women to believe in themselves, in their own truths and feelings—to remind women around the world that their feelings, experiences, and intuition are true and valid.

Our mission has always been to bring women to believe in their own magic and abilities. You see, we are all alchemists in our own right. Yet our magic and essence have been under attack, much as they were during the Salem witch trials. Women suffer as a result of their silence and passiveness every day. If you see this pattern in yourself, here is the sign you've been waiting for. You aren't crazy; you aren't asking for too much or doing too much or too little. You are magic, and that little voice in the back of your head is Spirit leading you. Don't ignore her, and don't silence her.

Nobody tells you how intense it is to become a human mother cow responsible for sustaining a growing human for the first one to three years of its life. This work should be honored and praised. On the same trip I just described, we also went to breakfast with my BD's junior high basketball team. I was exclusively breastfeeding and also adjusting to converting into a full-time life source for my calf—I mean, my baby. As I was eating, Luna began to get fussy and hungry, too. I was about to lift my shirt up to feed her at the table when my very old-school, conservative mother-in-law stopped me in my tracks and told me to go to the restroom. I was stunned but submissive. I got up from the table wanting to cry. Was it inappropriate for me to think it was a good idea to whip out my titty at breakfast in front of ten teenage boys? Maybe, but I felt even dumber locking myself in the public restroom at a diner alone to feed my baby. All this shit seemed too difficult to understand. Weren't boys of all ages supposed to learn and understand that women breastfed babies and there was nothing sexual about it? I felt I'd behaved oddly inappropriately by almost feeding my baby at breakfast, but I didn't really understand why.

These incidents were just small events in a bigger picture, and they slowly planted seeds of resentment, anger, and immense sadness. Many straws went ignored, and none broke the camel's back. Even as I am forced to relive this portion of my love story, so much seems lost. I had gone for years repressing, rationalizing, and managing my pain. I avoided feelings so often that it had become second nature to me. Putting myself last felt like the first lesson in motherhood. To be a good mom was to be self-sacrificing. But what happens when you put yourself last all the time? You lose yourself. And what happens when women lose themselves? They become resentful without understanding why. They become angry, bitter moms, wives, and friends and unrecognizable versions of themselves.

When society tells you to be one way and you conform to the role, you begin to perform instead of live. Performers are not supposed to parent—people are. When you perform, you inevitably teach your child that performing is an option, that denying your own feelings is okay and normal.

How you parent is in many ways your living testimony to your children. By showing up in ways that are not authentic to yourself, you teach your child it is okay to show up in ways that don't reflect their real selves, in order to gain others' acceptance.

Teaching our children to perform teaches them not to live from heart space. I consistently express to Luna, "I am human." I want her to understand and know that Mommy is human. I cry, I fuck up, and I hurt. I have no desire to show up as a superwoman for my child all the time, because I am not a superwoman. I try my hardest, and sometimes I fail. However, I always get back up, and she sees that, too. I've cried on Luna's shoulder; I've held her hand when I needed help. I've let her know that Mommy is a real person with real feelings, and by validating my humanity I inevitably give her permission to always be human first, too.

My vulnerability in parenthood creates a strong woman in training, who understands that she is powerful and she can also be imperfect. Because, hell, we are all imperfect beings, just attempting to grow and be the best versions of ourselves. If we as women and as mothers could give ourselves permission to be imperfect, we could collaboratively change the world. Giving so much of ourselves to others without boundaries creates turmoil. But what happens when we love ourselves? What happens when we give ourselves the opportunity to cry, to hurt, to heal, to pause, and recalibrate? Loving ourselves is our true superpower.

I've discovered that as mothers, we've normalized nurturing and giving grace to our children and romantic partners, but never to ourselves. Our children fall down, and we pick them up. They have a hard time learning something, and we gently teach them, over and over again if we have to. They "perform" less well than we expect, and we offer them words of encouragement and affirmation. We love them unconditionally, through and through, without question, but somehow forget to mother ourselves with the same compassion. Being gentle with ourselves seems small but is monumental in so many ways. Why is it so difficult to love ourselves the way we love our children? After all, we are the reason they exist; aren't we ourselves worthy of that kind of love? So often we seek for others to love us in ways we can't even love ourselves. It's honestly absurd. How can we expect gentle love if we haven't even conquered nurturing ourselves? I'll tell you why: because we don't feel worthy or deserving of it. When you don't take time to practice self-love, you will not know how to access it. You can go your entire life seeking it without first creating it. This is through no fault of our own, though; most of us didn't grow up witnessing our mothers set boundaries or engage in acts of self-love or compassion.

As a child, I experienced my mother showing up in ways that weren't true to herself as a sacrifice to her children. I got to witness firsthand what it looks like for a woman to lose herself as a result of attempting to be a superwoman. Not only did I witness this, but more than anything I felt it. I felt her pain, I felt her agony, because that's what our children do; they feel us. Even when you think you're concealing your shit or saving face for the family, you're not. Children may come in not knowing how to communicate verbally, but they do come with an immense amount of emotional intelligence—a sort of psychic level of sensing when things are good or bad. My distinct childhood memories of those feelings have always guided me in not insulting my child's emotional intelligence. I talk about my feelings often, as practice for me and guidance for her to always do the same.

That's what I like to call the authenticity factor—being honest enough with yourself to admit when something is wrong. It doesn't have to be some grand "problem" for you to feel as though you need to move on or move things around. Being authentic with yourself requires you to honor yourself in every aspect, even when you grow faster than your partners or close friends. We would like to believe that proximity to toxicity isn't contagious, but it is. Sure, we all grow at our own pace; however, the company you keep does affect you, both negatively and positively.

As humans, we thrive and grow in company. We truly need people—and not just any people; we need people who genuinely understand, accept, and love us. By recognizing "the God" in you, you can see that you don't have to feel guilty about being dedicated to yourself. Being dedicated to your higher self and to your growth is a far grander lesson to your child than staying complacent in your own growth while attempting to facilitate someone else's. The thing about true partnership is that it waters you, pushes you, and inspires you to expand because, in order to grow a family, you have to also be committed to your own individual growth. If you don't honor yourself, you're not honoring your child. Looking back, I can acknowledge that my desire for comfort was deeper than my desire for what would actually nurture me. I was comfortable in misery.

Being authentic means choosing yourself, and one summer day, after privately obsessing for close to two years about how stuck I felt, I asked BD to move out. I can't recall some specific, crucial event that caused me to finally put my foot down. I had just exhausted all other options and was finally tired enough to move on. To be honest, I didn't think that BD would willingly remove himself from the house that we shared, but Spirit moved him for me.

It was a Friday, and I wanted to go to my friend's bachelorette party. BD was abrasive about me going, which was expected, but I was drowning and desperately needing to come up for air. I told him I was leaving, and when I came back on Sunday, his things should be gone. I spent the entire drive to Palm Springs worrying and obsessing over my decision. I knew it would change everything. I was scared but also optimistic about what my future looked like detached from my relationship.

Surrounded by my friends, I felt the most "myself" I had felt in a long time. We drank, danced, and participated in all the traditional bachelorette debauchery. We went out that night and randomly discovered a team of young, buff semiprofessional football players who happened to be training in Palm Springs. We of course invited them back to our crib for a barbecue the following day, because how else were we going to find eight young, fine, straight, and strapped athletically built men in the infamously gay desert? The team came over and barbecued as invited, and when they arrived, I was topless (yes, I'm a nudist) in the backyard and decided I didn't feel like getting dressed. In fact, I didn't feel like appeasing anybody's feelings or comfort but mine. I had spent the past five years appeasing a man, and I did not have a single ounce of energy left for that shit. I knew some of my friends wouldn't be pleased, as they subscribed to the idea that one friend "looking like a ho" meant all the friends were hoes. Still, I didn't give a flying fuck. I knew some of the men might be shocked and might even make some assumptions. But I gave zero fucks, because I had allowed my relationship to deplete every fuck that I ever had to give.

Surprisingly, everybody survived. In fact, one young man in particular joined me in the Jacuzzi and respectfully praised my freedom and affirmed that very few women were like me and willing to show up as themselves. That gentleman didn't know it at the time, but his praise was what my soul needed—a gentle reminder that being untraditional didn't mean that I was a ho or for everybody, lies my BD had drowned me with over the years. This gentle giant of a stranger saw me, in my entirety. He understood the woman that I was, without judgment. I couldn't have needed that recognition more than I needed it that day. In some odd way, this man's conversation was the affirmation my spirit needed to remind me I had made the right decision. There were, in fact, men who still loved, admired, and appreciated women living in their truth and living authentically.

CHAPTER 5

POST-TRAUMATIC
Baby Daddy Disorder,
a.k.a. PTBDD

The men in the life of a girl or woman, whether she is straight or queer, shape how she views herself and loves herself. When we explore the roots of our complicated relationship with self-love, we uncover how male figures in our life have impacted us. For many women, post-traumatic baby daddy disorder is a big source of pain and trauma. The aftermath, when your family structure has not manifested the way you envisioned, is heartbreaking, but there is light after the dark. Promise.

ERICA

First comes love, then comes marriage, then comes baby in a baby carriage. That's not all, that's not all, now you're single—fuck them all.

Yes, they say the best way to get over someone is to get under someone. I don't disagree, and I definitely did that—but we haven't gotten to that chapter just yet. After a breakup, and after crying and feeling bad for yourself, comes a series of realizations that you willfully chose to participate in the fuckery. Not only

> ## Affirmation
> I forgive you, not to offer you peace, but to allow space
> for love and light in my beautiful life.

that, you've probably chosen this type of fuckery before, because we are creatures of habit. This is not to discredit the love I'm sure you shared with your previous or current partners. I very much enjoyed many parts of my relationship to my daughter's father. We had fun, we laughed, we loved each other, we traveled. But the aftermath of our relationship's demise did a number on me. Trust had been broken in a way that I wasn't sure how to get back. The idea of being in a relationship seemed impossible. Love was completely off the table, and my intuition felt as trustworthy as a dollar-store pregnancy test. I started going to therapy, and the inception of the podcast also served as very real wake-up call that I had a track record for loving a certain type of human.

So who is the prototype? Well, if we're talking physical features, he's gonna be tall, dark, and arguably just a little less than handsome. I decided in high school to rule out pretty boys, because all the girls liked them and I didn't feel like competing. I also thought, in my shallow mind, that if men weren't that pretty, they wouldn't take me for granted. Hello, insecurities! Now if we're talking about the foundations of a man or boy, well, alpha male is always going to win. Someone who can shift the energy in the room with his presence. Someone good at what he does. Someone people respect and fear. Someone who doesn't give me too much attention but who is possessive enough. A man's man, who reserves his vulnerability for me.

If you've heard of the five love languages, then you know that we typically have a hierarchy of a few different ways we want to experience love. I believe that most of us want a little of everything, but typically, each of us finds some of these languages to be more important than others. Historically, my love languages rank in the following order: physical touch, quality time, words of affirmation, acts of service, and receiving gifts. My preferred love language at twenty-two was different from what it is in my midthirties. My needs and wants have changed. I've checked certain traumas and nurtured starving parts of my soul.

The foundation of how we want or know how to be loved comes from childhood. Our parents, whether biological or not, are the first people who show us what we should accept or tolerate. They are our first loves. What a fucking terrifying responsibility.

I'm the product of a single mom. That wasn't the plan. But neither was any of this. My mom and my dad met in the early 1980s one night at a club in Los Angeles, when my mom was a beautiful twenty-three-year-old bright-eyed girl from Orange County and my dad was a twenty-four-year-old country boy from Sealy, Texas. Although young, they both had lived fantastic lives before they met. My mom had traveled the world a few times over with a few uber-wealthy boyfriends, and my father was at the height of his NFL career. They frequented the LA nightlife scene and had become friendly with none other than the legend himself, Rick James. Yes, Rick James, bitch! Rick played matchmaker, and so began their love story. Unfortunately, it didn't end the way most love stories do—or maybe it did. We all know nothing lasts in Hollywood, and neither did my parents' relationship. You guessed it: pregnancy, followed by a nasty breakup and a public DNA test. My mom was left to put together the pieces of a life she had never expected.

I don't have a super clear memory of the first time I met my father. He was at my birth and then sporadically in and out of my life as a baby. During one of my first therapy sessions, I had a very clear memory come up that felt so real. I was around three years old, and my mom had brought me to my father's football game. It was a bit chaotic as she carried me through the tunnel leading up to our seats. The next thing I saw was a huge field with players running and my mom pointing as if to show me who my father was. Next, she is holding me over the railing where the players run back into the locker room. I hear her calling for him. She wants him to look at me—the baby he won't acknowledge. He looks up, I catch his gaze, and he keeps running inside with the rest of his team.

I asked my mom about this memory, and she told me that she wasn't sure if this had happened. She told me that the hurt, pain, and straight-up code-switch my father did on her during her pregnancy made the first few years of my life a blur for her in some ways. She had blocked out a lot of the memories that were points of trauma, and she said she wouldn't have been surprised if she had forgotten something that was such a vivid memory for my little-girl brain.

Her experience confirmed how powerful the mind is when protecting a person from reminders of pain. You can never really re-create to a T the way something felt after time has passed. Sometimes the pain is so unbearable that, to survive, you must erase it from your memory. Dissociative amnesia is what therapists call it. We call it post-traumatic baby daddy disorder, a version of PTSD, because the trauma associated with the father of your child hits differently from a normal heartbreak. There is so much more at stake, especially if you were in love. However, we all know nothing is really "erased." It's always there lurking in the background of your life, showing up in ways you don't even notice. It can change how you date, how you love again, how you parent, your self-confidence, how you have sex.

For women, the loss of the family dynamic we are programmed to aspire to is fucking deep. We are hardwired to want to keep our families together—to tolerate problems and to "trust the process," because no relationship or family is perfect.

My mom was going to be a football wife, and then suddenly she wasn't. She wasn't going to live in the mansion on top of the hill. In fact, she was going to live in a small apartment in the Valley. She and my dad weren't going to be a happy family. Instead, they were going to be at odds for the next twenty-four years of their lives.

Since my dad was in and out of my life, the first confirmed memory I know to be true is from when I was about five. I knew who he was when he came to pick me up in his fancy sports car, but he made me nervous. He was basically a stranger I knew I loved without even knowing him. I was excited as my mom got me dressed and walked me out to his car. She gave me an envelope full of my doodles to give to him. I remember sitting in the back seat, a little nervous that I had left home with this stranger dad but also excited to see what his life was like. I stared at the back of his bald head and watched his eyes in the rearview mirror. I did look like him—so much like him.

We went to the bank, and he told me to wait on the couch. It was raining outside. I watched this stranger, my father, talk to the bank teller. It was the first time I had seen him interact with anyone other than my mother. He was charming. I wondered whether he loved me. I already loved him. We got back in his fancy car, and he took me back to his house—the mansion on top of the hill—and he showed me to my room.

His house reminded me of *Beauty and the Beast*. It was four stories, with what felt like ten bedrooms. I felt the emptiness and grandness of his home all at once. My dad lived alone in the little mansion he had bought for himself and my mother once upon a time. His house was immaculate—perfectly clean, everything organized. My Virgo father. This house was not for kids, and neither was my bedroom. He hadn't prepared the room for me. It was as if it was a room for anyone. It was a beautiful room, but it wasn't *my* room. I put on a brave face and acted as though I wasn't scared to sleep alone in my king-size bed, but I was. I had never stayed with a man before. Yes, this man was my father, but I barely knew him.

I wish I could tell you more details of this time or the times to follow, but they were very few and far between. My father, although charming and charismatic, didn't know how to make a little girl feel loved—to feel important or like Daddy's little girl. I wanted his attention, but he didn't know how to engage with me for long periods of time. Instead, I watched a lot of television.

Over the years, I began to learn what his interests were during our sporadic weekends together. I was a natural athlete like him, and it seemed my talents excited him. I was competitive by nature but secretly also thought that being good at sports would make him closer to me—that my proximity to his passion would bring us together, that if I showed him that I shared his genes, his DNA, he might love me more.

In my dad's autobiography, he shares a moment that I vaguely remember as a little girl. I asked, "Daddy, do you love me?" Even as a child I was unfiltered. Most children are.

"Of course I love you. Why?" he answered.

"Because you never say it." It was true.

Isn't it amazing how, even before the trauma sets in, kids have this special gift of calling it like it is? No fear—just the facts. As he reflected on this moment one day on the phone with me, he told me how deeply what I said had affected him; he told me that I was right, and he was wrong. He vowed to always tell me that he loved me, and he did. But words and actions are two different things.

I'm not here to say that my father didn't love me or doesn't love me. I'm here to say that he loved me as much as he possibly could, based on so many factors. One major factor was his childhood. Although as a child he was surrounded by a loving family, he grew up as a Black child in the Deep South in a small town during the 1960s, and much of his existence was about survival—not getting killed, making something of himself. Life was about not getting in trouble, and love was shown through cooking or harsh physical punishment, because it was better for kids to learn at home than out there on the streets. Black parents run their house on fear, because respect is king in our households, and the world will not be kind.

My grandmother gave birth to my dad at thirteen, and his entry into the world was filled with love but also lies. Until he was twelve years old, he was told that his mom was his sister and that his great-aunt was his mother. His teacher casually broke the news to him one day after school, and 'til this day he says this revelation did not affect him, but how could it not have? He had spent his childhood telling his "sister" not to boss him around because she "wasn't his mama," when in fact she was. The first women in his life had lied to him, and I've seen his lack of attachment to women and love throughout my life, in various relationships, including the one with my mother. He told me at a very young age that he had never been in love with my mom or with any woman, except for one girl in high school who broke his little heart. This admission broke *my* heart, as I would sometimes daydream and romanticize what my parents' short-lived love story was like. If he had never been in love with my mother, did he have the capacity to love me deeply?

I feared him. How could I not? I didn't know what made him tick.

I didn't know what made him uncomfortable besides me using the Lord's name in vain or running in his house. I didn't know his favorite foods or favorite color. I didn't really know much about this man who had lent his DNA to my existence, and as a young girl I didn't have the language or the bravery to ask too many questions. I just knew I wanted to be in his presence and that I felt a connection to this stranger dad of mine. I knew I felt protective of him, and even as a kid, I could pick up on the ways certain people felt about him on my mom's side of the family. They were wrong—until they weren't.

My dad gave me doses of attention. And when I got those doses, it felt like Disneyland, I wanted the attention so badly. But kids grow up, and I was a mature child. I began to pick up on my dad's serious shortcomings around age seven. My mom never spoke ill of my father, but I could feel her pain when he didn't show up to pick me up, and I began to see how inconsistent he was. Going to school will also show you the different family dynamics that exist, and mine wasn't the standard. Kids would share stories about what their dads did for them that weekend or even talk shit about their parents. I had nothing to share, because I would often go months or even a year without seeing him. To be honest, reflecting on my childhood now as an adult, I, much like my mother, blocked out many of the painful parts of how I felt. I know he didn't come to pick me up often, didn't show up to games, and didn't call on holidays or birthdays. I credit either my mother making sure I was quickly distracted from my disappointment and my post-traumatic stranger father syndrome kicking in during those moments.

By the time I was a teenager, I had stopped making excuses for my father's absence, and the hurt and pain were poignant. I couldn't talk about how I felt about him without immediately sobbing—literally. I had suppressed my feelings so much growing up that when they surfaced, I could feel my throat close and body tense, and uncontrollable tears and emotions followed. How could this man whose exact face I stole not want to be a consistent force in my life—not show up for me or treat me like the daddy's little girl I saw in the movies? The last straw happened on my sixteenth birthday, and I decided to cut him off after so many years of suppressing my hurt and pain. I hated him (not really), and I felt I didn't need a father anymore.

The years of wanting his attention had already begun to affect my need for adoration from boys and my subconscious addiction to choosing ones I had to chase. I mean, let's be honest, dating as a teenager is kind of a reflection of how you were parented. I knew that I had a strong voice and powerful presence, like my mother, and that my skill of attracting attention was one of my superpowers. But I often misused these powers. I found myself in "serious" relationships but unable to stay faithful because I did not know how to curb my need for male attention. I never had ongoing talks with my mom about boys and the way I should be treated or how I should treat them. I say "ongoing" because, as a parent now, I realize that these types of conversations deserve to be revisited more than once, twice, or even three times. When it comes to uncomfortable or "taboo" topics, it's important to come back, check in, evaluate, and readjust, so that children feel heard and empowered to make their own choices.

I lacked confidence in my own self-worth and tied much of it to how many stupid boys liked me. Eventually, I began to grow out of being a serial cheater and was myself cheated on by my much older music producer boyfriend. He made me feel special because I was young, and he was older; I felt chosen by this semisuccessful man who played games better than I did. When that relationship ended, I chose a colleague at my record label internship to be my partner. He was nerdy and protective, and he didn't trust me at all. He went through my phone constantly. What they say is true: if you look, you're always going to find something you don't like, and, boy, did he. To be honest, I wasn't physically cheating, but I still had a strong need to flirt and be desired by other men, even though I loved him. Surprisingly enough, he didn't like that very much, and so that relationship ended in a fiery shitstorm of verbal and physical abuse.

Daddy issues were playing out in real time. What does a girl with suppressed daddy issues do next? Jump into another relationship.

It had been three months since my epic breakup with record label bae, and I had been flirting with baby daddy over texts. He sent me sweet notes telling me how he put me on a pedestal and how I was the most beautiful woman he had ever seen. Next thing I knew, we were moving in and building a beautiful life together. Yes, my daddy issues were still intact, but we had a genuine friendship and partnership that I had never felt before. For the first time ever, I had zero desire for anyone else's attention. But we're not here to dig into the fairy-tale romance I experienced for the first two and a half years of our relationship. We're here because after the honeymoon phase is over, life starts life-ing, and shit gets real.

As I mentioned in chapter 1, one of the dynamics of my relationship with baby daddy was that I constantly had to support him emotionally because there was always a tragedy, panic attack, or wrongdoing happening in his life. The natural nurturer in me wanted to be there for him and took pride and joy in the fact that I could support my man through moments of vulnerability and chaos. When our relationship ended, I realized how much time I had spent in that space, always worrying about him and whether his panic attacks or enemies would come for him or us. When he moved out of our house, I was terrified to be alone. I had become accustomed to feeling unsafe in my home, and now that I was a single woman living alone, every time the hardwood floor creaked or there was a rustling in a bush outside, I felt my life was under threat. I was extremely paranoid because he was extremely paranoid. Even now, after many years of knowing nobody is coming to get me, I still have this fear about my physical safety.

I also have noticed how difficult it has been since that relationship for me to accept male vulnerability in my dating life. The stress of always worrying about baby daddy's mental well-being has affected how much I am willing to support male feelings; I almost run at the first sign of them. Therapy has helped me identify my "daddy issues" and "PTBDD" that both of the major loves of my life left behind for me to sort through. Trusting that a man will stay and be loyal to me and my feelings is hard for me to believe, although I want to. Everyone says I can find that trust: "Just hold out, Erica, your person will show up when you least expect it." I'm not expecting it, and this unicorn man they talk about hasn't arrived. Maybe it's me and all my "issues."

I've had to take long looks in the mirror and ask myself what role I have played in these relationships. Over the past few years, my father and I have healed many parts of our past. I don't hate him, and I never did. I fucking love that man so much. Forgiving him meant also acknowledging and working on the ways I've treated men in my life based on the expectation that they were going to disappoint me. I had a reading done by an incredible intuitive who asked me, "What happened on your sixteenth birthday? Whatever it is, you need to forgive your father for it, or else you will continue in this cycle of love and disappointment." I couldn't believe she knew to ask that question, but I also couldn't believe that I still carried disappointment. I thought I had moved on, but after talking to my dear friend and master well-being educator Devi Brown about the reading, I realized that my sixteenth birthday was the day that I had stopped trusting not only him, but all boys and men.

After this confirmation, Spirit inspired the exercise that follows, which has been transformative for rapid healing in my relationship with my father. I encourage you to try it in the practice of forgiving anyone in your life. This is a great exercise for those who can't achieve the forgiveness or receive the apology they desire because the person who hurt them is incapable, toxic, or dead. Not to be harsh, but often we need to forgive people who, in reality, don't feel like they owe you shit. In the case of me and my father, he did apologize a few times, and I thought I forgave him. But when I found that I was still experiencing some triggers, I knew I had to do the rest of the work myself.

I barely made it around the first corner of my walk without sobbing while practicing this exercise. I did this for weeks, and eventually I made it around the block. It would have been crazy to have had to repeat these things directly to my father the number of times I had to say them out loud on my walks before genuine forgiveness finally broke the surface. Imagine calling him every day to do this—it would have been absurd! But I had to speak my forgiveness out loud countless times so that I actually believed it and could release my pain.

Despite the experiences we have in our childhoods, it is our responsibility to transmute our pain into understanding. Victimhood isn't cute, sis.

Walk It Like I Talk It

Decide which person you are focusing on forgiving. Go outside and take a walk. As you walk, begin talking to the person. I started forgiving my father by starting from the beginning.

"I forgive you for abandoning my mother
when she was pregnant with me."

"I forgive you for not coming to pick me up
countless times you said you would."

"I forgive you for not showing me what my worth is."

"I forgive you for not asking me how I felt or
not apologizing for not showing up."

"I forgive you for not making me feel like Daddy's little girl."

"I forgive you for making my mom cry in
my arms when I was four years old."

"I forgive you for not being there the
first time a boy broke my heart."

"I forgive you for not teaching me the life lessons a father
is supposed to teach his daughter and protecting me."

MILAH

Of course, because I am the overly compassionate Cancer that I am, baby daddy's moving out was still not my true "final straw." But at the time, it was my first big, desperately needed step in the right direction. For a lot of women, the first step is often the hardest. Feeling stuck in a toxic relationship is a paralysis that is almost impossible to describe when you are in it. It's just as hard to witness from the outside looking in. I had experienced years of abusive behavior from my BD, much of it verbal. I endured this abuse in silence, unaware of how much it had begun to deeply penetrate my spirit. I had vented and confided in my friends time and time again, but at some point they got tired of hearing me complain without taking any real action. Hell, I was tired of my complaints and complacency.

I threatened him often, "When I'm done, I'm done. You will regret how you've treated me, and I promise you, I will never look back." He didn't believe me. Neither did any of my friends. I was dead-ass serious, and I knew I wasn't lying. Once I made the step, there was no way I was coming back. But like many women, I had to live out the breakup in my mind a million times first. Visualizing all the possible scenarios was the mental preparation I needed to finally make it real. I would move, but when I was ready to move—or actually, more like when I was completely fucking depleted, exhausted, and deep into depression.

You know us women, we love to give a muthafucker 56,655,758,758 opportunities to get it right before we can believe they no longer deserve us. At that point, I was somewhere

> ## Affirmation
> ### I forgive myself for choosing other people's safety over my own.

between a sunken place and checked the fuck out, because BD would respond with comments like, "Do you know how lucky you are to have the opportunity to be with me? I'm a god!" No, for real, that's a direct quote; I can't make this shit up. He had definitely begun to go off the deep, manic, Kanye end. Again, this is not an attack on anyone who is suffering from mental illness, but it is a warning to anyone in an abusive relationship: certain shit is simply unacceptable. We as women are always trying to save a ho, and some hoes just can't be saved. What's more, it's not our responsibility to save everyone. We first have to be willing to save ourselves. The "put your mask on before assisting others" rule is real as fuck and applies in life, not just on airplanes.

Verbal abuse is scary because it attacks your spirit in an inconspicuous way. There are no physical bruises, blood, or wounds. Years and years of mental warfare can leave scars on your confidence that you don't even recognize until you are stuck and depleted. Most of my friends were relieved when baby daddy finally moved out, but none of them could understand why I hadn't put my foot down sooner. They were tired of my shit, as I was, but when you're in it, there is no logic. Even as rational as I am, I couldn't understand the amount of patience I had extended to this person who could not extend the same.

None of my close friends had kids at the time, so naturally

they couldn't truly relate to what I was going through or the attachment I was battling with. I desperately tried to explain to them my understanding that he was bad for me but also my delusional hope that he would "come around." These explanations were useless because they had no merit. Like many women, I had this unrealistic hope and expectation that some magical lightbulb would turn on, and he would suddenly come to his senses. After he moved out, I thought something would click, and he would become the man I hoped he could be. I thought he would realize how close he was to losing his family and would somehow want to show up differently. His moving away was a major step but did not create a strict boundary.

I was slowly learning to exist independently with a two-year-old on my own. Changing pace was both rewarding and intimidating. To be honest, it was lonely—which was odd because I had previously been miserable with his company. I had become so accustomed to the pain that I had learned to exist with it and was actually attached to it, so much so that existing without him was uncomfortable. We still did things "as a family," because I subscribed to the idea that if we didn't do family things together we would fall into the broken Black family stereotype. So I was doing shit to please complete strangers because I was attached to an idea that I hadn't created for myself. Although he had moved out, he still had access to my emotions, which meant access to my overall well-being. He was out of my house but not out of my life.

Despite not being very religious, I was all too familiar with one prayer. I reserved it for emergencies; it was a prayer for God to intervene and have his will be done. I knew that, of all the prayers, this prayer worked. When you know you need to exit stage left, and you've exhausted all other options, as I had, that is when you call on the final prayer: "Please, God, if this isn't for me, make it so clear that I don't have a choice but to walk away."

This prayer was far more powerful than Ciara's prayer for Russell, because unlike Ciara's prayer, mine wasn't calling in a person. In fact, mine was a prayer of releasing, resetting, and healing—powerful because it was calling in truth. If you prayed this prayer, your spirit was already aware that something in your calibration was off and in need of a shift. As women we will endure some shit; we will make excuses and hurt ourselves for the love of our families, for the "family structure." But when you pray this prayer, be prepared to honor yourself and God's will.

It was late. I had just left a client, so I met my baby daddy out at a bar. He had been drinking with friends, and so I drank, too. I often opted to drink when he drank, so I could tolerate the environment. The more he drank, the more I drank. I seemed to think that if I could get on his level, then maybe I could forget how unhappy we were. On this particular night, everything was fine—I thought. We started to drive back to pick Luna up from my best friend's house. I ran in to grab her and get her things, but apparently, I took too long, because when I got back to the car he was in a rage; he was always kind of in a rage. He sped off before I could get her in the car seat so, of course, I reacted.

"Stop the car!"

"Why the fuck would you take so long, Jam?"

"Please stop the car so I can put her in her seat."

He just continued to drive without stopping. We argued the entire way to his parents' house. I tried to grab him to get him to pull over, but I was scared. Scared for my baby, scared we would get pulled over, scared that he didn't understand or have limits when it came to jeopardizing our child.

Even as I am writing this, I hesitate to include this part of the story. As transparent as I am, as honest and "real" as I am, this has been painful—to exist in, to exit from, and now to revisit. I hesitate to tell my truth for fear that the world may think I hate men or that the man I once loved so desperately would see me as an enemy. But censoring my story, as a last attempt to protect my "family" and the father of my child, would be a disservice to myself and to you. The truth is, shit happens; people are flawed and fuck up. We hope that we grow and learn from those mistakes, but unfortunately, not everyone does. People who don't aren't necessarily bad people, but to keep your peace you may need to avoid them.

"If we are silent about our pain, they will kill us and say we enjoyed it!"
—ZORA NEALE HURSTON

Someone gave me a piece of advice I never forgot: "Would you want your daughter to date the person you're dating"? That shit sank in. The truth was, I'd never sign off on my daughter dating someone like who my BD was at that time. So as I sit here and resurrect this portion of my life, I hope you can understand that no matter the person or circumstance, it is never worth it to make excuses for someone's bad behavior; it neither heals nor helps. As I share with you my experience in motherhood, it's so important that we understand motherhood in every sense—the motherhood we experienced in childhood and the motherhood we embody now, as well as the parenting our friends and partners have experienced.

As we continued to drive that evening, he became more and more enraged. I shut down, as I had so many times before, but this time it felt different; he seemed to be even more off the deep end than usual, as if he had checked out and someone I didn't even recognize had taken over. He pulled into the driveway of his mother's house, and we continued to argue as I held Luna; then I felt the back of his big-ass hand quickly strike the bridge of my nose. It happened so fast that I didn't even really feel it. But then I touched my face and looked down at my hand, and I realized it was covered in blood. One hand was holding Luna, and one hand was covered in blood. I was completely in shock. What the fuck had just happened? Was I in a fucking *Lifetime* movie? As panic flooded my mind, the garage door lifted; his parents must've heard the commotion from outside. As I got out of the car and approached his parents in tears and in shock, I could see their faces react to mine, and I knew I wasn't trippin'. His father looked at me with utter disbelief.

"What did you do?" his mother asked him as she took Luna from my hands and I proceeded into the house to assess the damage myself.

When I got to the bathroom, I was shaking, and my heart was racing. I took a look in the mirror at my bloody face and bloody hands and thought to myself, *This is not my existence. This is not my life. I didn't sign up for this shit.* Of all the shit I had ever tolerated, I never imagined that I'd be the victim in a domestic violence scene. I felt like the main character in a bad Tyler Perry movie, getting assaulted by my baby daddy with my baby in hand. What the fuck?

I was in shock but had a moment when I made eye contact with myself in the mirror. This was the first time I had really looked myself in the eyes in a long time. It dawned on me that this might have been my doing. It was that goddamn prayer. I'd asked God to make it so clear and so unbearable that even I couldn't make excuses for my baby daddy, and here I was, looking dumb as hell, battered in his bathroom—in the house he grew up in, where we had so many childhood memories of falling in love. In some ways I had asked for this; I know in any other circumstances I would have found a way to pacify and make excuses for his behavior.

Everything that happened next was kind of a blur. I attempted to call the police, but when they answered I became frightened and riddled with guilt. I still couldn't be honest. I had been trained never to involve the authorities with a Black man, even if that Black man just beat your ass with your small child present. As the phone rang on the other end, I stood face-to-face with my BD and his mom and dad staring at me, waiting to see what I would do next: blow up his spot or hang up. The operator on the other end of the phone answered, and I froze—then hung up. The phone rang moments later as the operator called back: "Ma'am, did you mean to call this line? Is it an emergency, can we help you?"

"I'm okay," I answered. I wasn't okay, but I couldn't be a snitch.

"Are you sure, ma'am? We received a phone call from this line."

Without hesitation, I said "Yes," trying to conceal the tremor in my voice. Again I had let him off the hook—still attempting to protect him even though he had abandoned all pretense of protecting me or his daughter.

That ordeal was the straw that broke the camel's back, but I still hadn't given up all hope for him. His hitting me was, however, the sign I needed. I definitely never saw myself as a victim, especially not a victim of domestic violence; this reality was far from what I had ever imagined my reality would be, but here I was living it. Crazy. I had experienced trauma all this time, but seeing my blood that way truly put a fire under my ass and made me see the relationship for what it was—abusive. Why did it have to become so extreme before I chose to really disconnect? Was I a dumb bitch? How had it come to this? When the fuck had I become so lost in love that I had lost my actual self-respect and intelligence? Sure, there were signs, but this felt extreme.

Truth is, there were many acts of abuse all along, but for me the sign of blood made me wave my white flag. This was the moment I started to really detach emotionally. I finally was forced to acknowledge that it wasn't up to me to heal him; even if it had been, I didn't have the tools to heal him, because Lord knows I wanted to. It was the first time I acknowledged that someone who didn't want to be healed could not be healed, no matter how much love, sweat, and prayers I put into it. No child, no tears, no conversation, no therapy sessions could save a man who wouldn't acknowledge his own pain.

That night, I let Luna stay with his parents; I called an Uber and went home to try to process what had just taken place. But what I really had to process was that this behavior didn't just start that night. I had to actually acknowledge the abuse I had endured for years, which had all led up to this point of realization. I was on edge, battered, embarrassed, ashamed, and honestly stunned. Even now, almost five years later, I'm still spending some time processing that encounter. It's true what they say: You don't become a victim overnight. It's a long, drawn-out process. Little attacks of abuse finally accumulate to some big act, until what you've tolerated makes you not even recognize yourself.

After that night, I was afraid of him but still hopeful he would finally see his ways and be remorseful. But his apologies were half-assed, and of course he argued that I had pushed him to that point. One thing about narcissists is that they are never responsible for doing anything wrong, even when there's literally blood on their hands. I was slowly dying, cut by cut. Even though these cuts didn't bleed physically, they still made me feel as though I was slowly bleeding out.

For months after this incident, I slowly made more distance between us. I stopped relying on his help and "friendship" and began seeking companionship elsewhere. But even that wasn't easy. BD was obsessed with me and sometimes called me sixty times in succession, even if I didn't answer. He would start with my phone, and then make his way to the inboxes and call logs of every one of my friends.

One night I invited a guy over. I found myself securing my blinds, windows, and doors out of pure fear and paranoia. I felt oddly guilty for having male company. Looking back, I see that my paranoia was valid. I was scared of BD and in constant fear that he was watching me—for good reason, because he was, in fact, watching me. I was in my second-floor apartment when I heard some noises outside my window. Something told me it was him. I plunged to the floor and directed my company to do the same. I crawled to the next room, in a cold sweat with my heart racing, when I heard my bedroom window slide open.

My heart fucking stopped beating in my chest, and I froze in panic. Every scenario crossed my mind. Was he coming to kill me? The guy, someone I didn't know that well, got up immediately, opened the door to my bedroom, and found my BD hanging out of my second-story window, about to attempt to climb his big ass into my house because I hadn't answered his calls all night. Still, I was frozen like a statue in the next room. My stomach was in knots as I could hear this guy asking my BD, "What the fuck are you doing hanging out of the window?" I don't know what else was said, but I did hear my neighbors open their window to see what was going on, which apparently scared my BD, because he jumped down and left.

As absolutely psycho as this story may sound, I can't make this shit up. After that I couldn't sleep, I couldn't rest; my heart was beating out of my chest until that guy left the following morning. Still, I somehow felt an immense amount of guilt. Had I moved on too quickly? How had I dared to have company over so soon? These crazy questions were a direct result of having been gaslit for an extended period of time. I blamed myself when it was clear and obvious that my BD had lost his shit.

After that night, it took me months to feel safe in my house alone. I constantly felt I was being watched and followed. I confused that behavior with love instead of seeing it for what it was, more abuse. I had been concealing and making excuses for his behavior for so long, but when other people got involved and also witnessed it, I was reminded of how not normal it was to have to go through the shit I was going through.

At that point, I had to really start severing my relationship with him. I finally started to choose me, because choosing him was not only hurting me, but it was also actually causing me to be high-key delusional. That's the thing with being in a relationship with someone suffering from mental illness: you will fuck around and start to actually feel crazy, too. I never wanted to be alone, so I mostly kept roommates to help me with rent and to feel semisafe.

I hope this painful story can serve as a reminder that normalizing fucked-up behavior never has positive results. Making excuses for people never resolves their issues; it encourages them and hurts you.

CHAPTER 6

I'M SINGLE—
Now What?

Many of us have grown up with this idea that we will meet Prince Charming, fall madly in love, and get a ring and a house with a white picket fence. All the good stuff is what comes in between those benchmarks, but still we jump straight to matrimony and babies.

Literally, at birth, we start giving little girls kitchen sets, baby dolls, and strollers, almost as if to say, "Welcome to Earth—here's what you need for your future destiny." But what if you don't want babies, or marriage, or even a relationship? Or what if you do want babies, but not a man? (I mean, have you *met* men?) Or what if you want marriage for now, but maybe not in a few years when you discover he's cheating on you or the spark just isn't there anymore? The point is, marriage and the baby carriage aren't every woman's damn destiny. And, in fact, every mother's "normal" looks different.

ERICA

I'm a statistic. I'm a statistic.

That's what I kept hearing over and over again in my head. Another Black mom whose baby daddy cheated and ended up with an accidental baby—yup. I'm a statistic. I should have just joined

Love & Hip-Hop: Hollywood when they asked, because clearly, I fit the mold perfectly.

These were the thoughts that still sometimes consumed my mind when I let myself sit still too long. Seven years, complete with an engagement and a baby, all resulted in me becoming a single mom—my biggest fear. All my life, I had watched my mother tirelessly try to balance single parenthood, career, and life. She did it with grace, but I still told myself that would never be me. I would do it differently. I would show her that, even though my baby daddy wasn't who she'd dreamed of for me, I would still succeed at creating a healthy family structure.

Welp, I was wrong. There I was, in the wreckage of my relationship, and I was left thinking that I should have cheated. Or at least I should have kept a few old lovers in my back pocket. Instead this loyal Scorpio was faithful AF and had zero rebound options. Was I even appealing anymore? I hadn't felt like myself in the three years since having my daughter, let alone looking like the Erica I once knew. The exhausting work of taking care of my child and my relationship had been the greatest reason in the world to neglect my dreams, my goals, and myself. I felt lost, with no direction about what fulfilled me in work or pleasure.

One day I was having lunch with a friend, complaining about my ghetto love story, because that's what women do when they are hurt or angry: they talk about it all the time. Hearing other people tell you what a piece of shit your ex is feels good. On this day, my friend wasn't having it anymore. She grabbed my phone and said, "Enough already. I'm signing you up for Tinder."

"Tinder? You mean a dating app?"

The only dating apps I had heard of were for lonely old people, Christian singles, or mail-order brides. She assured me that the dating app scene had changed over the previous seven years, while I was "wifed up," and that I should go get my feet wet. I was skeptical but also had nothing to lose—except my pride and privacy. What if someone saw me and told my ex? What if someone from high school read my profile and shared it with everyone we used to know?

Fuck it. She was right. I did need to get my feet wet, and maybe some flirting would help get my confidence back up. I reluctantly began adding my pictures and building my profile. How does one sound fun and carefree in a few sentences? This is how:

About me: LA native, Scorpio, potty mouth, tequila, feed me tacos, may not call you back, here for a good time not a long time.

I adjusted my search setting to a very small perimeter and started swiping.

Dating apps are interesting. You get to see how people want to be seen—what they think matters to other people—and the type of people who are interested in you if they feel they have nothing to lose. I was surprised at the different types of men who found me attractive: white, Middle Eastern, Asian. All my life I'd only ever dated Black men. Could Tinder help me broaden my horizon?

Getting my feet wet was exactly what I needed. With every "super like" and flirty message I got, my confidence increased. Maybe I still got it? Maybe I am "fine AF"! Sean with the green eyes and plethora of gym photos seemed to think so. I soon became obsessed with checking out the app and flirting with men I knew I'd never meet. A few weeks went by, and my friend asked if I had gone on any dates. I hadn't.

"*What?* Why?"

I had no answer, except that it seemed creepy and scary to meet a man off the internet. She looked through my messages and saw that I had been talking to a handsome guy named Matt for the past week.

"Him. You're going on a date with him."

He was Black and wore glasses. A vet working as a photographer, he seemed sweet; our banter had been entertaining and fed me the validation I needed.

"Fine."

I dropped off Irie at my best friend's house and told her I'd be back in two hours. I figured my first date would include a drink and some small talk, and then I would call it a night. I met Matt at a small, dark tiki bar in North Hollywood. I was late, of course, and I saw his body get tense as I walked toward the table. That's when I knew he was exactly what I needed. His eyes lit up as I sat down, and he stuttered a bit as we started running through the usual get-to-know-you small talk. He was nervous, and I fucking loved it. I took control of the date. I was going to make this man fall in love with me, because that is what the doctor ordered.

It happened to be karaoke night at the place we were at, so I confidently went up on stage of the almost empty bar and sang "Tyrone" by Erykah Badu, because that's what you do when you want men to know you don't play that cheap shit. He watched me in awe, and I felt my sex appeal fill up my body like a thermometer in a well-done turkey.

After a thirty-minute make-out session in my car and a little finger fucking, I sent Matt on his way. I knew I'd never call him again. He was too timid but exactly what my soul and body needed to remember that I was a bad bitch.

I dove in headfirst. I started using the app when I traveled for work, and I had a few domestic and international rendezvous I'll save for another time. In short, what I realized was that this new way of dating allowed me to pick and choose men in a way I never thought possible. It also allowed me to tap into exploring with women in a way I was too scared to do in the past.

I had had a few sexual encounters with women before my baby daddy showed up. I had even flirted with the idea of bringing women into our relationship, but the lack of trust threw that idea out of the window. So, after a few fun dates I decided to indulge my curiosity and open up my sexual preferences to all genders. Not having to guess if a woman you're attracted to also likes you is part of the magic of exploring your sexuality on apps. I became excited by the idea of possibly dating a woman. I mean, why not? All the cool kids were doing it, right?

One night as I was swiping in boredom, I stumbled across a picture of a beautiful woman with a face carved out by Black

Jesus himself. I swiped to see another picture of her in a bathing suit. She was fine. I swiped again, but this time it wasn't just her in the image. She was kissing a white man in front of a temple. Next was just a picture of him. Hot—and I don't really do vanilla. I went on to read their profile:

"Married, adventurous couple . . . looking to spoil you."

I sat there for a while wondering if this was real. They were both so beautiful. Maybe it was fake. Could I fuck a married couple? Do I fuck both of them? What are their rules? I held my breath and swiped right. "It's a match" popped up on my screen. Fuck.

They were real. We quickly got off the app and onto a group text, where I got a crash course in how they navigated their marriage, parenthood, and a unicorn. For those of you who don't know what a unicorn is, here is a definition:

u · ni · corn (noun): a person who is the sexual guest in an established relationship

Yes, they had a toddler and were still DTF other people . . . together. Kissing was cool, condoms were a must, and staying in group communication was a hard rule. We flirted, they sent me sexy videos, and I did the same. They were easy to talk to and made me feel comfortable and sexy. We finally decided to meet. They picked the spot: a little Mexican restaurant in Reseda that was discreet and low-key.

I asked the nanny if she could babysit Irie at my house and

got dressed. I wanted to get there early, and I did, which never happens. I started to drink. I was nervous. I decided before I got there that I would let them lead. They walked up to the table, and I couldn't believe it. They looked even better in person! She was curvy and soft, with beautiful skin and big curly hair. Her husband was handsome, with a gorgeous, goofy smile. We chitchatted about the weather and the food as I sucked down my strawberry margarita like a Slurpee.

For the sake of their privacy, let's call them wife bae and hubby bae. At some point during the conversation, wife bae laid her hand on my thigh and started to caress me. I was immediately nervous but happy that she had made the first move; I was too scared. Her touching me under the table in a public place in front of her husband shot electricity through my body. I wasn't sure whether the night would lead to intimacy, but now it was clear they came here with intention. Before I knew it, I was following them back to their house. As we sat on the couch smoking, wife bae leaned over and kissed me as hubby bae watched. Her lips were soft and full, and her tongue gracefully slipped between my lips in a way that said, "We're fucking tonight."

Before I knew it, we were all making out and touching. We stumbled upstairs to their room, where they undressed me and laid me down gently on their bed. I knew I was in for a treat and that their profile description ("looking for someone to spoil") was accurate. They both settled between my thighs and worked together to bring me to pleasure. She took control and told him what to do to me, and it was clear her goal was to make sure he did everything to please me. Hubby bae and

I loved on her while they stared deeply into each other's eyes. Their connection combined with their care and attentiveness to me made me feel in awe and honored to be a guest and audience to their love.

When it was over, we laughed and kissed, and hubby bae walked me to my car. We said goodbye with our tongues, and he sent me on my way. As I drove home, I felt exhilarated. What the fuck had just happened? That exists? Trust like that? Married people? Good parents can still fuck other people and be happy?

I had always imagined what it would be like to share and explore sex with a partner I could trust. I had finally seen it in action. I was a part of it. That was the moment I knew transparency in love was all I'd ever accept moving forward. I had just witnessed it, and it was real. I arrived at my house, and my daughter was still awake. Mommy had just had a threesome, and now it was time to read a bedtime story. I giggled inside at the irony of the evening. I felt empowered by my decision to explore my sexuality and also this intangible sense of pride at being a mom who got home in time to tuck her kid in.

Am I saying join Tinder and find a couple to sleep with? Maybe, if that's your thing. The real lesson here is that dating as a single parent doesn't have to be black and white. You don't have to date to find the next love of your life. Go have a few flings and make a few bad choices that feel really fucking good. Ignite the ho deep inside you've suppressed for years while trying to be the trophy wife to your partner. Explore your fantasies, and get excited that you get another chance to redefine what pleasure looks like to you.

What's Your Fantasy?

What are some of your wildest sexual fantasies? They can be as vanilla as flirting with the barista at the coffee shop and secretly making out in the bathroom or as naughty as fucking the fine-ass single dad in the empty classroom during parent-teacher conferences. Write your fantasy down in detail, and visualize it. If you are partnered, what are some ways you can start creating new rules or experiences in your sex life to heighten your pleasure? Get excited at the idea of surprising your lover with something new and sexy— maybe lingerie or a new sex toy.

If you are single, what are some healthy ways you can explore your appetite for pleasure? Maybe you'll use a dating app, swipe on all genders, and have flirty conversation. Or maybe you'll find a sex party in your city and go with a friend, as a voyeur or participant.

Sometimes the healing is in the hoeing. Sometimes it's best to heal first and hoe later. Only you know what you need, but either way, it's a whole new world, as they sang in *Aladdin*.

But unlike that Disney movie, this story doesn't begin with white lies, and an arranged marriage. Absolutely not. And you, my dear, do the choosing.

The options are endless, and there is no shame in exploring your deepest desires, mama. Wouldn't the real shame be in never exploring them and dying an old, shriveled-up shell of the sex goddess you coulda and shoulda been?

The answer is yes. That would be a shame, and we ain't doing that, sis.

MILAH

After a few mellow dramatic *Lifetime* scenes, not much had changed. My BD still lived the same lifestyle he did before: he drank heavily and was mean as hell and oddly competitive when he refused to even apply for a job.

Being pregnant and having a baby had changed me at my core. I knew I didn't deserve this treatment, and I certainly knew this situation could not be my be-all and end-all. Yet, still fighting my intuition, I did everything in my power to "fix" our relationship. I talked to his parents and demanded we go to therapy. I even prayed about it, and to be honest, I rarely prayed. I asked God to change him and heal him. One night I was so desperate, I laid my hands on him like a reiki witch doctor and attempted to telepathically transfer words of hope and affirmation to his body during a home massage.

My friends would bring up their concerns about incidents of clear disrespect they witnessed in my relationship. In response, I would just become annoyed and eventually shut down and disappear, time after time after time. To everyone, it was clear I was miserable and in denial. I was aware but wasn't ready to accept

Affirmation
My life, my muthafuckin' rules.

that yet. Even though my heart had spoken, my ego was screaming, crying, and kicking to hold onto this nonexistent fairy tale.

I sunk deeper into depression, without ever acknowledging it as such, in an attempt to avoid becoming a stereotype. I took to endlessly scrolling on Instagram, looking at all the strangers who had had babies around the same time as me, beaming in motherhood and taking happy family photos with their perfect families and perfect partners in their perfect houses, and I would feel angry. That was what I was supposed to have, too!

"Why, God, why can't he just . . . ?" I asked over and over again. The longer I sat in my relationship, the more apparent it became that nothing was about to change, and slowly I internally came to terms with reality. I started "strategizing" my exit plan and visualizing what being single as a mom, after a breakup, would look like. The daunting thought of becoming a "single Black mom" was almost as horrifying as choosing to be in an unhappy relationship, but I knew I had to leave the relationship—if not for myself, then for my daughter.

Here I was, two years into motherhood and just getting into a "groove," and I was being forced to shut down my lifelong dream of embodying #familygoals to figure out what single motherhood looked like, for real. I couldn't just kick him out the house and then continue to act as if we were in a relationship, as I had been doing. That meant not depending on my BD for anything—small or big. It was time for me to actually cut ties and act like a single woman. Would I be allowed to indulge in casual sex? Were there any men who would want to date me now?

I watched the future I once saw for myself slipping away. The thing is, I knew I still wanted marriage, which meant diving back into the dating world, and this time with the "baggage" of a baby daddy. After all, in the women's handbook of unwritten rules, having a baby with someone only to end up single is at the top of the list of don'ts, especially if you want a chance at a relationship again. If I'm really being honest, according to the Black women's handbook of unwritten rules, becoming a single mom is equivalent to failure. In fact, I'm pretty sure the term "baby mama" was created to place single Black moms in a box, also occupied by Halle Berry's character in the movie *Losing Isaiah*. Even though I'd known and met many single moms and knew that they were often great, hardworking women who were single by choice, it was hard to unlearn the stigma. For decades, the depiction of single Black moms has included poverty, welfare, ignorance, and being ghetto.

But once I was actually in that position myself, I realized that I was actually already surrounded by outstanding "baby daddies" who genuinely loved me and respected me. My best friends were already my baby daddies, helping me with childcare, supporting me emotionally, encouraging me, buying things they noticed we needed. Once my community saw that I needed out, they rallied around me, surrounding me with love and support. My parents were local, and during a time of need I was able to lean on them and my friends.

It turns out, I wasn't a statistic at all. I was loved, I was encouraged, and I was a strong Black woman who had generations and generations of strong women inside me who had survived much worse circumstances and still made it. I tapped into these ancestors and pulled from the pain and strength of my grandmother, who had to raise three children alone after my grandfather left for the babysitter. I pulled from my own mother's pain, watching her stay in a marriage with my dad just because they, too, had dated since childhood. I took her fear of walking away and used it as my motivation to do things differently. I leaned into the African proverb "It takes a village to raise a child," felt blessed to have a village, and finally let go. In changing my perspective—one that had held me captive for years—I liberated myself from a limited mindset. But once I emerged on the other side of my relationship—shaken yet intact—I realized I still had not the slightest clue of how the fuck one navigates singledom with a baby.

It took months after my baby daddy left, but I had finally started to settle into my apartment without him. I dried my baby mama tears and bought a few things on Facebook Marketplace to renew my spot and make it more my own space. One weekend when he was with the baby, I wanted to indulge in the guilty pleasure of having full days and nights off from mom life. I decided to fully utilize my free time and my space alone. I hadn't been in real close quarters with any man outside of my daughter's father for five years, and the idea seemed so unfamiliar and foreign. Having a late-night visitor on my temporarily free weekend made me feel as if I was in high school all over again, doing something naughty, sneaking boys over when my parents weren't home. At the same time, I was eager to get my feet wet and consummate my singledom. (*Translation:* I was horny for some new dick.)

I could've fired up Tinder or another dating app, but I wasn't in the mood to banter with a stranger and waste time trying to figure out whether we were a good match. I wanted someone I knew would be down. So I finally responded to that tall, dark, and handsome Egyptian man in my DMs, Mark. I had first seen Mark at the nail salon my friends and I frequented in the neighborhood. I noticed him immediately because he was a fine-ass man in a nail shop, which is a pretty rare sight. After that first sighting, I started to see him there more and more often, and I later learned his family actually owned the overpriced, posh franchise. He was quiet and sexy, with dark olive skin and dark features. He looked like someone Hollywood would cast to play a pharaoh in a film, complete with a six-pack, a dark mole beneath his eye, dimples, and a beautiful smile. We flirted every time I got my nails done. Yes, Mr. Egyptian Nail Village had been on my list of to-do's for some time.

One random late night I had been hanging at a local bar with my best friend's baby sister and her friend who was visiting from out of town. As we stumbled out of the bar, we met a couple of guys outside and drunkenly crammed into their Uber to find food. We finally arrived at a late-night Mediterranean hookah hangout, The Spot, that's been a staple in the Valley since before I can remember. When we arrived, I was tired and over being out, but I hadn't been anywhere after midnight in a while and didn't want to be the party pooper. We sat at the table with two guys who weren't really my speed and began to look at the menu. While I was still fake examining the menu to avoid conversation, I heard a third friend of the guys walk up and join us. I looked up, and to my surprise, it was fine-ass Nail Village Mark. Immediately my temperature rose and the butterflies in my stomach started up. So funny how the presence of an attractive man can send a woman's energy up a wall in a matter of seconds. He sat down, everyone introduced themselves, and I mentioned that we had met before at the Nail Village. When he didn't recall meeting me, I also mentioned a few of my friends who got their nails done more often to jog his memory. He looked at me and said, "Oh yeah, you have a baby girl, right?"

I replied in the affirmative, smiled, and immediately sank into my chair and let the mean girl in my mind take over. I felt so insecure, and negative thoughts clouded my mind. Being out at 2 a.m. with a group of hot male strangers was once a regular weekend routine for me, and suddenly it felt not just foreign but incredibly daunting. I hadn't done my hair because it was longer than it had been in years, and my YouTube natural hair care routine wasn't a routine at all, so I had thrown on my Erykah Badu scarf as a means to cover it up. Now I was sitting at a table with a fine-ass man feeling ugly and insecure as shit.

Suddenly, in my peripheral vision, I saw Mark, who was across the table from me, stand up and begin to walk around the table. Maybe he was going to the bathroom? But he seemed to be coming . . . Straight. Toward. Me. My heart raced, my stomach dropped, and I began to sweat. Mark picked up a chair from an empty table and slid it up next to me.

Ohhh myyy God!

He sat down, leaned in toward me, and said, "I'm really sorry I didn't remember you at first—you look different. But I remember you now. How have you been?"

I was shocked but kept my cool; I might have lost my inner

mojo, but my ego missed no beats. I'd never come off as anything other than calm, cool, collected, and flirty. Milah hadn't lost her groove that easily, and with each passing moment, smirk, and laugh, mama was slowly getting her confidence back.

He asked me about Luna and life and never left my side of the table. We exchanged Instagram handles, because that's what the kids are doing these days, and after our early morning dinner ended, I got in an Uber home with a little extra pep in my step. Within minutes after my departure, I noticed a DM from Mark that read:

> Was really nice to run into you and talk to you tonight, let's keep in touch . . .

The message was followed by his phone number. I could have passed out. I felt like a schoolgirl, grinning like the goddamn Cheshire cat. I was still attractive to fine guys, and I could still hold my own! It was the beginning of the unburying of the old Milah I had missed so dearly, and I was ready for her to reemerge.

Mark was one of those guys who is strikingly handsome but in a humble, quiet way. He was bashful and had a soft way of flirting that made you question whether he was actually flirting. At thirty-three, he still lived in his parents' house because of some strict religious rule that permitted him to move out only once he was married—which, in an odd way, made me even more curious about his religious dick and also left me with little expectation that this crush would turn into anything too deep.

After our initial Instagram DMs, we had been to a couple of yoga classes together, but tonight, a few weeks after we had first met at The Spot, I was forward. I invited him over. When he walked in with takeout, I knew it was definitely going down. I was a little nervous but mostly I was horny and feeling myself, so after a little smoking, a glass of wine, and some small talk, my fangs began to emerge. Apparently his did, too, because bashful Mark was no longer so bashful—or holy. He grabbed the back of my head and pressed his tongue deep into the back of my mouth, in a way that almost made me choke. He slid my hand over his pants so I could feel the hard bulge in his pants grow.

I immediately got wet. Mark must've sensed a pussy alert, because he removed my pants, then my panties, and licked me like a starving alley cat. He turned me over, tossed my body over the arm of the couch, and continued while occasionally coming up for air to smack my ass, hard. I responded by being hella dramatic and moaning loud as fuck because *nobody was home to tell me shit.*

I turned around and mounted Mark, and he removed my top, exposing my big, beautiful, post-baby engorged breasts. As I gave him my best sex-kitten bedroom eye and passionately made out with him, I tried not to become distracted by his balding head, which I had never really seen without a hat on it. Still moaning as loud as I could, Mark went to suck on my neck and then my breast—until I remembered: *Oh shit! I'm breastfeeding.*

(*Insert screeching brake noise here.*)

I had no choice but to grab his head back and whisper, in the most sexy voice I could muster, "Be careful, you might get some milk," while cringing and bracing myself for his response.

I felt him grow underneath me. Nasty, religious Mark responded, "Then let me taste that milk, baby," as he eagerly suckled at my erect nipples. Needless to say, I was turned all the way on. My neighbors got a porn-star earful that night.

I sent Mark home after a couple rounds of passionate, no-strings-attached sex, and I suddenly felt that my situation was not, in fact, the end of the world. Being a newly single, new mom didn't seem to make me any less sexy or desirable to men. These new developments in my life, far from deterring me, started to empower me. As a new mom, I knew I would have less time for shenanigans now that I had a daughter to take care of. I knew I could navigate the dating space better, as I had less time to waste on the bullshit. And after surviving a relationship that tried to break me, and with a daughter I needed to provide an example for, I felt like a ninja ready to knock out and kung-fu any fuckboys who tried to throw any bullshit my way. My perspective shifted, and I discovered a beautiful disconnection that allowed me to indulge in my pleasure without all the guilt attached. I had spent months putting myself in a box of do's and don'ts as a new mom, and one sex appointment was all I needed to feel good about myself again.

The moral of my story is this: Do what you gotta do; make your own rules. Living a life to please others will not bring you pleasure. Have the one-night stand, use the dating app, stay out late. There's no age limit for fun. You deserve guilt-free pleasure. I think the kids use the term "YOLO"—you only live once—and they're right. Seize the muthafuckin' moment, mama. You have been given the gift of life. Don't forget to live yours!

CHAPTER 7

MAMA GOTTA
Have a Life, Too

Pleasure and joy are synonymous. Exploring personal pleasure is a road map to discovering personal happiness. Don't underestimate the power of accepting and owning your mind, body, and soul. In a society that is constantly telling you who you are, it is revolutionary to own your bliss.

ERICA

As I settled into my singleness and the conscious choice that I was and would continue to be a single parent, how I decided to spend my time became more of a question. I didn't have a day-to-day partner in the house to give me breaks from my child. I didn't have certain luxuries that partnered people have. Now, before the married or partnered people reading this get all up in arms about being stuck with all the responsibilities of parenthood in their households, I just want to say that my experience isn't here to minimize yours. I am aware of the partners who don't step up to help with the daily activities and responsibilities of raising a human. However, if you are putting up with that treatment, this is a conscious choice you have also made. No shade, but tell that husband to do his MFing job. On the days that I'm sick or tired,

> ## Affirmation
> My pleasure is a priority. I must fill my cup first.
> The overflow is what I give to everyone and anything else.

I don't get to take an hour off unless I hire someone or lean on my family or friends for help. Often single parents must push through or tough it out and treat their happiness or health as an afterthought.

Not only was I nursing a sometimes aching heart, but I was also nursing two humans: my child and this new person I was giving birth to—myself. This was a turning point. Life shifted for me, and I could make decisions solely based on what was best for me and my child. I had another opportunity to rewrite the rules of life and motherhood. If you are coming out of the ashes of a breakup or major shift, get excited! This is the best part— the time you get to try everything. It's like throwing away your entire wardrobe and going on a shopping spree with unlimited funds. Pick up everything you like and return what doesn't fit or suit you. Your childhood traumas don't disappear, but you do get to decide how they show up moving forward. You have a new lease on life, and you're only leasing that bitch for twenty-four months, because you're not investing more time in things that don't drive well or make you feel good.

With all that said, I went through waves of feeling extremely liberated in my newfound freedom and then feeling extremely isolated and alone. I felt empowered knowing that I could get shit done and accomplish things as a single parent that I had relied on my partner for or hoped he would do before. Simple things like taking out the trash, assembling furniture, and driving my daughter to her various activities in one day made me feel like a good fucking mom for doing it alone. Even though there's so much power in being the primary parent, every supermom has to take that cape off sometimes. But how?

When my daughter was still an infant, I was scrolling through Instagram and saw my friend post somebody named Jamilah. She was posted up in her bikini with a drink in hand and her tiny baby on her hip. I thought to myself, *Wow, she's living her life.*

I knew I wanted to meet her. I messaged our mutual friend Nisha and asked where she had been hiding the only mom in our friend group. She laughed and told me to meet her and other friends at a local bar in Hollywood that night. I dropped my daughter off at my mother's house, jumped in the car, and headed to the bar. I had one mission: find the skinny bitch with the baby. I looked around as I grabbed a drink and mingled with friends I hadn't seen in a while, but I knew I didn't have a lot of time to find my future friend. Where was she? I made a beeline for the bathroom, and she was there touching up her makeup in the mirror. I got straight to the point.

"Hey, you know Nisha, right? I heard you have a baby, too."

"Yeah, I do!" She was friendly, thank God, because this wasn't my usual MO, and I was nervous AF.

"Cool, I think our babies are the same age. We should get together!"

We exchanged numbers, and I left for home immediately, ashamed about leaving my daughter to go to a bar and worried that my mother would judge my choice to go out on a weekday.

The next morning I texted Jamilah, and we made plans to meet that weekend. After she arrived, we made margaritas and got in the pool with our babies, who could barely hold their heads up. This was clearly a playdate for us and not them. We talked about our relationships and put on a brave-ish front. We weren't ready to spill our guts but were happy to be doing something for us. We smoked behind the garage because we were at my grandmother's house, and God forbid she should see me smoking weed and have a newborn. It was exactly what I needed to feel normal, even if just for two hours. After that, our hangouts were few and far between. However, I still kept up with Jamilah via social media and saw that she was still living her life, which gave me permission to do the same, unbeknownst to her.

When Jamilah invited me to Luna's third birthday party, I couldn't wait to tell my wildest mommy friend that I had joined Tinder and was exploring new relationship dynamics on my own terms. Mama had gotten her groove back, and my pleasure was becoming more of a priority to me. Somewhere between cutting the cake and opening presents, I had told Jamilah about my new married couple, and her face lit up with excitement. She had just finally really broken up with her BD for the last time, and I, her sometimes mommy friend, was with the shits.

Much as with our first encounter at the bar, I had another motive for coming to Luna's infamous birthday party—"infamous" because this was the day I proposed that Jamilah and I start a podcast together. I had been listening to murder mystery podcasts for months, but when I searched for shows about single motherhood, there weren't any. All the mothers who were doing podcasts were very Caucasian and very married; the conversations of these wine-drinking moms barely scratched the surface of my experience.

"Like a radio show?" asked Jamilah, as she carried the princess-themed cake through the party.

"Kind of, except it's not live. We would just sit down and talk about motherhood and our dating experiences."

She was down. Jamilah is always down, and thank God, because I needed her in more ways than one. Our connection was one I was going to keep, and I was ready for a new best friend. She had a way of making me feel safe, she had smart and strong opinions, and she was fucking fun. Our sometimes friendship had given me the courage to make space for myself, and I think she felt the same way, even from afar.

> **"As we are liberated from
> our own fear, our presence
> automatically liberates others."**
> —MARIANNE WILLIAMSON

What I've learned from our friendship in the five years since that fateful birthday party is that every mom needs a friend she can take her mask off with, maybe get drunk with if that's her thing. I was just tapping into the space nearly a year after my breakup and really starting to understand what it was that made me happy outside of my child—how I wanted to spend my precious time. Wasting time is important, too; you don't know how you want to spend your time until you've wasted it. It's the polarity of your choices that eventually guide you to the answers you're looking for and the things that feel right to you. I knew I wanted to sit down and hang out with my new single-mommy friend. For me, it was guilt-free fun, because we could connect, talk our shit, and smoke our weed, all while the kids played in the other room.

During the time when I started my friendship with Milah, I started to unpack the toll of guilt that single parents feel when they don't want to have a kids' playdate and do want to just live for themselves and enjoys life's simple pleasures.

Even the most empowered woman still struggles with guilt, because as women we have been told to make our own pleasure second to everything else in our lives.

Speaking of pleasure and shame, when was the last time you looked at your vagina? Have you ever looked at it? Like, *really* looked at it. Fuck it, even if you have, go get a mirror. I'll wait . . .

We often wait for a man to explore our bodies before we do. We look outward instead of inward. When you become a mother, you're told that your child is your world—that choosing yourself is selfish, that dropping your kid off at your parents' two weekends in a row is unheard of, and that taking a two-week trip to find yourself is blasphemy. If you're a mom, making any bad choices could potentially ruin your child's life, so you tiptoe around and avoid yourself completely.

Somewhere along the way in my relationship with BD, I became extremely unsexual. At first, I attributed this to pregnancy, then to my weight gain and not feeling sexy. It got to the point where I thought that I no longer wanted sex at all and never

Isn't She Lovely?

This exercise may feel unnecessary or make you feel uncomfortable. Good. That means you have work to do. Now, pull down your panties and look at your vagina. She's beautiful, she is. I know you may be carrying shame about what she's supposed to look like, but fuck all that. She is gorgeous, and you should tell her. No, for real. Say it out loud. Yes, it feels strange, but we have to get in the habit of talking nicely not only to ourselves in the mirror but also to our bodies. Let's be honest, ladies, our yoni (the Sanskrit word for "the womb" or "the source") is the portal of life and deserves to be revered by its owner. If you want to step it up a notch, try self-pleasuring in the mirror. It's fucking hot.

would want it again. I had been so hypersexual most of my early adult life that I hardly recognized myself anymore. I would make small promises to myself that I would prioritize my pleasure and masturbate when I got home, but I would either fall asleep or write that idea off as unimportant. During the first few months of my singleness, I started to see the woman I had been before. I needed to feel good again, so I wore sweats less and put makeup on more. I had felt undesirable and questioned my worth so much that I had forgotten how damn fine I was. I slowly began to peel back the layers to see the Erica I once loved. Yes, she was still insecure and a lotta bit broken, but she was a little more powerful. Giving birth will do this. I remember going to a sex shop for the first time after becoming single again. I hadn't bought a vibrator in years. Why would I? I was basically asexual, and real dick was in my house. I pulled into the driveway of the Romantix sex shop in my neighborhood and debated whether I would go in. I hoped that whoever was inside wouldn't ask me any questions, and then I wouldn't have to explain why I was there.

I'm here because I have no sex drive and no sense of what my personal pleasure is anymore. Can you help me?

The Erica I know today would march right in and ask all the questions, but this version of myself was embarrassed that any stranger would know that I might be contemplating my own pleasure. God must've been listening, because after I walked in, no one said shit as I strolled the aisles. My nervousness turned to excitement, and I grabbed the strongest and smallest toy I could find. I paid and quickly got out of there, and when I got home, I lit every candle in the house and set the mood as if a lover was going to be joining me. That lover was me, and I made the rules.

That night, I experienced an orgasm that I'm sure had been waiting deep inside my body for years. I was safe, and I realized that this was the disconnect between me, my body, and my former partner: I didn't feel safe with him. I didn't trust myself, because I was semicomplicit in his cheating, by forgiving him and allowing him continued access to me. My orgasm that night was different from a mutual exchange. It was about my personal pleasure and reclaiming the sensual woman I knew I had always been. In the words of a guest on our podcast, Devi Ward Erickson, a Tantric practitioner, "Pleasure is our birthright."

A GOOD MOM'S GUIDE TO MAKING BAD CHOICES

Experiencing myself intimately and alone was one of the driving factors of tapping back into myself. Masturbation became my self-care and my release, not only sexually but emotionally.

Being able to take control of my pleasure made me feel powerful, sexy, and desirable. It prepared me for dating or at least the possibility of exchanging energy with the opposite sex in a more nurturing way. This notion that prioritizing our pleasure over our children is irresponsible will have you judging other moms who do take care of themselves while you run on fumes. Nobody is saying "Fuck them kids," but we also *are* saying "Fuck them kids"—in the nicest, most loving way possible. You cannot pour from an empty cup, my love. You are no use to your children in a state of depletion, and I'm here to tell you boldly and loudly that your pleasure and joy matter. Your kids do not have to be the only source of your happiness. Read that one more time, out loud, for shits and giggles.

With this new good-mom hierarchy, I also began making more space for the things that had made me happy before I had Irie. In my late teens and early twenties, I had traveled the world as a personal assistant to a musician and had fallen in love with travel. I had planned trips with friends to music festivals and staycations in my prebaby life, but I felt that those days were over, especially now that I was a single mom. As I started to tap back into my personal bliss, I also started to tap into other activities that made me feel like the old Erica I once knew and fucking loved. Yes, I was the mom at Coachella drunk as fuck on the polo grounds, and it felt fucking great. We deserve to party, we deserve to make bad choices, and we also deserve to come home to our kids and be good-ass parents. I had never thought all those ways of being could exist together, but once I started to feel more safe in my body and my choices, I also began to take more risks.

I might have judged another mom who was doing some of the shit that I was now doing, but I was happy that I was experiencing this new awakening and this new friendship that I found with Jamilah. I was releasing the false narrative of what kind of mother I was supposed to be for my daughter and pushed through the inevitable judgments of family and friends with much anxiety but steady follow-through. Choosing your happiness should be easy, but it isn't—not in this world, where everyone thinks they're an expert. You and only you can decide what your happiness is. If staying at home with your kids for fourteen days straight brings you joy, then do that shit. I, however, am not that mom. I need breaks. I need a recharge. I need friends. I need solitude. I need quiet. I need weed. I need tequila. And I need my vibrator.

One tip I have for moms who feel shame around experiencing untraditional pleasures or wanting to take time for themselves is to not ask for permission. Many of us have the habit of sharing and asking advice from our biggest naysayers. These people can be your parents or your best friends. Stop asking them for permission if you actually want to live in *your* truth. Stop nurturing your fears with opinions or advice from people who have made you doubt your choices in the past. Protect your choices. Hire a babysitter and fire your parents if that's what needs to happen for you to have a night out on the town in peace. Now, I know all of this is easier said than done. Not all of us have the means to hire outside help, but if you really care about making your happiness king, then you will figure it the fuck out.

MILAH

I had completely underestimated the toll this five-year period had taken on my life. Experiencing the aftermath of that trauma, I started to slowly seek out some normalcy. I probably should have looked into some sort of therapy, but tequila, some forgettable men, and a new, jazzy haircut were much cheaper. I was just determined to get back to the old me, who gave a fuck about myself, my appearance, and my joy.

So much of my normal life had been on pause for so long, everything felt foreign: being home alone, going out, hanging out with friends. I was desperately seeking to feel human again, but I was in pain. None of my friends could understand the grief I was processing, and although they supported me through this breakup, they couldn't relate. As far as they were concerned, I should have been out of my relationship a long time ago, and they were right. But a breakup mirrors a death in many ways—the abrupt absence of a loved one. I literally had to go through the motions of grief and mourning the relationship.

Breaking up with someone with whom you've shared the creation of an entire human baby is something completely different from a regular breakup. I'm convinced that women develop some kind of invisible, energetic umbilical cord that is

Affirmation
I am a sexual and sensual being, and I deserve
to express my divine feminine power and experience
pleasure in every aspect of my life.

connected to their baby daddies, making it emotionally more traumatic and difficult to break free from these men.

Slowly, I started to find joy in the smallest "wins": taking out the trash, walking the dog, and putting Luna to bed on time made me feel as though I had conquered the world singlehandedly. But it took me some time to find "the old me," mostly because she no longer existed. I was a completely different person from who I was before motherhood, and I was definitely a completely different person after that relationship. At first, I was riddled with shame and fear of being viewed as a "ho"; my ex had done a hell of a job on my mental health, especially the image I had of myself. Even though I was longing to wild the fuck out and be a ho just to get back into the swing of things and rid my mind and body of all things baby daddy, I was lacking in the confidence department.

I was also just really lonely. I had made a few friends, but none I could really connect to. Honestly, I had practically forgotten about Erica during the two years since I'd first met her; I had been in the thick of early motherhood and the end of my relationship, and she and I had hung out only a handful of times since first meeting. I knew she was going through her own shit, and really, I was so ashamed that I didn't have the balls to reach out and say, "Hey, I need support, I'm sad." I wasn't used to feeling like the victim or expressing my needs to friends in that way. Allowing a man to treat me the way BD did made me feel like a weak woman, and I couldn't dare let anyone else see me that way.

Even though I wouldn't reach out, God seemed to know exactly what I needed when I needed it. On Luna's third birthday, somewhere between margaritas and cutting the cake, Erica and I had a brief conversation. Apparently, she, too, was going through a melodramatic breakup with her baby daddy. I had heard about it through the grapevine but didn't want to prowl too much into her business; when she disclosed this to me herself, I was sort of relieved. Finally, someone who understood what the fuck I was going through. Although by this time I was making my way out of the shadows of life with my baby daddy, I still desperately needed that kind of friendship.

After Erica shared her baby daddy's ratchet baby mama drama, she followed up with a story about a couple she had met on Tinder and was seeing. *Ding! Ding! Ding!* Now that was the story I needed to hear! I was tired of being depressed and feeling lonely. Quite honestly, I needed a partner in ho crime, and on that Saturday afternoon it appeared that I had found her. Since our first introduction, our lives had been a whirlwind, but looking back now, it seems to me we reconnected in divine time. I know this may sound strange, but Erica's story about this couple she was recreationally hooking up with made me feel human. Just knowing there was another single mom out here freely exploring her singledom gave me hope.

Finally, I wasn't the only baby mama in the crew, and I knew

Erica could understand the struggle and the disappointment of becoming a "stereotype"—an added layer to my experience that most of my non-Black friends could not relate to. I felt for her, but I was also excited to know she was both a good mom and a bad bitch, exercising her right to be liberated, fun, and sexual. Although none of my friends outright judged me, none of them were moms, and I knew some of my newly single "ho" experiences were privately being questioned. Some of my friends had subconsciously subscribed to the idea that I was supposed to be a conservative prude of a stay-at-home mom even after my breakup. After all, many of us women hold one another to this unrealistic standard without even realizing we're doing it. All I really wanted was a safe space where I could be free to show up as my full self without being judged; when Erica shared her story about the couple she was seeing, it seemed to me I had found what I was searching for.

At this point in my life, I was unlearning a lot of false narratives about what I was and wasn't allowed to do and be in relation to my pleasure. I had spent many years in my relationship with BD being reduced to "my ho activities" and being ho-shamed. Given BD's long history of creeping through my text messages, laptops, and journals, I was also left highly paranoid and self-conscious in the wake of our relationship. For me to have a casual, friendly conversation with someone of the opposite sex, in BD's eyes, meant I was "doing too much" and "being too friendly." Didn't matter who it was—our mutual childhood friend or an employee at the checkout lane at Target. I was in constant defense mode and had learned to avoid confrontation by any means necessary. Spending many years concealing parts of who I was to appease a man who loved women and loved sex but didn't want his woman to be overtly sexy was confusing as fuck!

I had been a rather sexual and sensual being ever since I could remember, but limiting parts of myself for that relationship had left me yearning to let my inner sex kitten back out of her cage. Growing up, I gravitated toward women who seemed to be un-apologetic about displaying this side of themselves; I saw this aspect of those women in myself, and I wanted to freely embody it as I got older. My mom was comfortable being naked in our home, but I didn't see her as someone who owned her divine feminine power, probably because the era she came from suf-fered from a Virgin Mary complex. Just as in our podcast episode with sensuality doula Ev'Yan Whitney ("Asexual and Sensual"), my mom had upheld the lie that my dad was her first and only lover. The relationship with my dad had clearly robbed her of her self-confidence, but she had been in that relationship for forty years, and I had been in mine for only ten. Watching her lose herself to a relationship made me cling to the pieces of my-self that so many had told me to abandon.

There are so many mixed messages pertaining to women, our bodies, and the ways we use them and express our sensual selves. What's considered acceptable? Who is "wife material," and who is not? I had spent many of my prime years in Atlanta carelessly expressing and exploring my sexuality, so it wasn't a department I was unfamiliar with. I had just temporarily lost touch with those parts of me, and hearing Erica openly talk about her plea-surable noncommittal sexual experience gave me permission to stop trying to fit into anybody's fucking box. I hadn't seen Erica as a "wild woman" like myself, and I was so relieved to discover that we weren't very different at all. I wasn't the wild, "out there," freaky anomaly that my BD had tried to make me out to be.

It's absolutely crazy how women's bodies have been policed—making it difficult to navigate our yonis because we're disconnected from the power of showing up in our feminine. We end up seeking permission to own the power of our own pussies. We literally have the power to make and birth babies, but we allow society to dictate the way we express that power when we blindly accept and uphold these rules around our bodies and sexuality. As creators of humans, we are innately sexual beings. It is in our essence to be both sensual and sexual. You cannot remove one from the other.

I believe that this attack on our sacred sensuality is a way to control our pleasure. When the way we experience pleasure sexually is controlled, we also lose touch with the ways in which we experience pleasure in all facets of life. The attack on our sensuality is a method of robbing us of our joy by disconnecting us from an essential aspect of our existence: our powerful, divine bodies.

"As women, shame creeps into our lives early and manifests in a variety of ways. Mostly in the way we carry ourselves, how much space we take up, how we choose to utilize our bodies and how we mother or don't mother. But you cannot shame a woman who is unashamed and unapologetic."

That day at Luna's third birthday party, I ended up celebrating more than three years of motherhood. I was also celebrating the conception of *Good Moms Bad Choices*.

Erica casually asked me, "Do you want to start a podcast?"

"What's a podcast?"

She could have straight-up asked me if I wanted to rob a cat on Mars, and I would have been down. I wanted to do anything with anyone who could relate to me. So I said, "Yes!"

I had one question and one question only: "Are you going to share the story about your Tinder couple?"

This was me asking, "Bitch, are we about to be honest or be fake?" I didn't quite say that, because we didn't know each other that well yet. I knew Erica was cool, but honestly, this Tinder story was the first indication that she was cool cool, and we just might be cut from the same cloth. She thought for close to five seconds before answering, "Yeah, I can't get fired!"

"Perfect! Me either," I responded.

The one thing I had managed to do during my roller coaster of a relationship was to finish beauty school and get an aesthetician license. I had worked something like five other odd jobs in the process, but eventually, I started my own small mobile spa business, because I didn't like being told what to do. Erica was a beautiful actress, and she worked for her mom's wildly successful global beauty business—well, that's what my friends and Instagram had told me, anyway. I'd be lying if I said I wasn't mildly intimidated, but nothing beats intimidation like desperation and loneliness.

I felt like a high school girl who had been chosen first to be the team captain—fucking ecstatic. I had been so bored and unfulfilled in my day-to-day life. I was desperately seeking something but had no idea what it was that I was seeking. Reconnecting with this friend who was also suffering from the life-changing breakup of a long-term relationship, and who also happened to be Black, was exactly what I needed. I would be lying if I said I wasn't surprised that she chose me. We hadn't been very close; in fact, we hardly knew each other then. Erica told me she had been listening to podcasts about crime and had searched for some on motherhood, but they were all very white, very married, and very dry. I hadn't dove into podcasts, but I had seen many white moms on Instagram—nothing I could relate to—so I knew she wasn't lying. So right there, on a Saturday afternoon at my daughter's third-birthday princess party, the seeds of the *Good Moms Bad Choices* podcast were planted.

Part 3

A REBELATION

CHAPTER 8

BITCH,
I'm Magic

Different elements of self-care and ritual can help you tap into your highest self—from plant medicine to manifesting. When you create intentional practices followed by action, you become unstoppable.

ERICA

Listen, sometimes you have to tap out to tap in. That means drop those damn kids off and go find yourself real quick. It's virtually impossible to focus on your healing in the presence of screaming toddlers or needy husbands. Everyone's "tap out" looks different, too. What's for me isn't necessarily for you. I like Flamin' Hot Cheetos. You might like Cheetos. However, they're the same brand, and they serve the same purpose—putting cheesy deliciousness in your mouth. That's how I feel about adult self-care. Do what makes you feel good. Do what works for you.

I was twelve years old the first time I smoked weed, and from my teens through my adult years, I have found ritual, peace, and communion with the cannabis flower. Like many teens and young adults, I dabbled in recreational drugs, and thankfully nothing else stuck. Speedy things worsened my anxiety and disturbed my

Affirmation
I am made of love; therefore, love will always find me.

naturally laid-back disposition. Plant medicine is more my vibe, and Mary Jane is my oldest plant bestie, who has supported me through anxiety, creative blocks, physical pain, and eventually happily playing Barbies for hours on end. She has become a ritual in my life and offers me balance and peace. To me, there's nothing better than a wake-and-bake before breakfast to get my day started or a nicely rolled joint before being creative, having sex, or doing anything else that's pleasurable. Cannabis has been somewhat of an anchor in helping me connect with myself and slow down my overthinking brain.

Once you have children, you start to realize how important self-preservation is and how difficult it is to get back to who you really are. You can start to feel desperate, disconnected from your body and your spirit. Maybe you start overmedicating or drinking too much. Maybe you stay out too late, to avoid being home. Or maybe you find every excuse to never leave the house. At some point, hopefully, you begin to understand how crucial balance is to rediscovering the woman you are. Many of us can attest to not even remembering who we were before we had children and then suddenly being faced with this little human looking up at you and wondering, "Who is mommy?"

I don't fucking know.

I dealt with this realization after having my daughter and feeling like a child myself. How could I be responsible for this baby when I didn't feel I was standing ten toes down in who I was? Of course, using drugs or plant medicine is not the only way to find out who you are. But plant medicine has accompanied me on my journey, helping me to strip back the layers, appreciate the present moment, and dive inside my unconscious mind.

So repeat after me: you have permission to tap out in order to tap in, and tapping out can mean smoking a joint or having a beer. Sure, bubble baths or yoga classes can be medicine sometimes, and they are great. But I'm here to legitimize other coping strategies that are often labeled "bad" and therefore can make us feel like "bad moms" for relying on them. You're not bad if smoking makes you a better version of yourself. I'm not exactly advocating for the "wine mom" life, but I am saying that women can be cannabis-positive while also being good moms.

For me personally, several plants, or "drugs" as the majority prefer to call them, have been a part of my healing journey. In addition to finding solace in my daily life with marijuana, I discovered shortly after becoming a mom that psilocybin (a.k.a. magic mushrooms) was one of the initiators in understanding the inner workings of Spirit without judgment. My long history of questioning my worth, body, and choices, paired with now being a mother, gave me crippling anxiety. I had trouble even ordering food off a menu without feeling overwhelmed.

The first time I took mushrooms with a real intention was in a little cabin up in the mountains with a friend. I was about one year past my breakup and still mourning the loss of that relationship while also trying to figure what the fuck my purpose was. Watching my parents and my friends strive in their careers made me feel inadequate. Would I ever figure it out? Every other time that I had taken shrooms, I had been at a music festival or a party, with my only intention to get wavy or fucked up. This time was different. My friend asked me to bring pictures of the people and things I wanted to let go. I remember packing my bag and sifting through old photos, some of myself as little girl and others as a young woman in love. Pictures have a way of holding you hostage to what isn't real. I was ready-ish to begin peeling off what felt like skin that didn't belong to me anymore. Something had to shift. I had never taken a trip with this friend or really hung out solo, but I felt called to say yes, in much the same way I had felt called when I dropped off Irie to meet a stranger in a bar. My soul knew before my mind did that something was going change up there in the mountains, and it did.

We took the psilocybin in its purest form—as dried-up, disgusting mushrooms. There's no getting around it: they taste like shit. Before we took them, we each said what our intention was for this journey we were about to embark on.

"To move on and release myself from the pain and disappointment of my choices. To feel better than I do right now and to find Erica."

Those may not have been my exact words, but essentially the message was, *Please, God, help me get over this shit and be the bad bitch I know I am.* We tapped the shrooms, chewed them quickly, and washed them down with OJ. They really do taste terrible.

About thirty minutes into our walk around Big Bear Lake, everything started to look more vibrant. One of the thrills of using mushrooms is the way it highlights the beauty all around us. Colors become brighter, and objects become more majestic. I looked up at the sky, and I realized how infinite the universe is and how small I was. My existence, although important to me, was not so unique. I wasn't the first person ever to have the love of her life have a baby on her. I wasn't the first person whose dad abandoned her. I wasn't the first person to experience any of this pain or joy. The idea of not feeling special was transformational for me. It sounds negative, but it was actually positive and allowed me to humble myself, to understand that my mere existence was a gift. Breath, legs, tongue—I had all these simple treasures that allowed me to wake up every morning and enjoy my life. Plant medicine will force you to surrender to yourself, Mother Nature, and the elements around you—making you feel connected to the people you share the experience with and grounded in your humanity. Can't we all use more of that?

After basking in nature and gratitude for hours, we went back to the cabin. It was time to release. My friend asked me to take out the pictures I brought. As I pulled them out of my bag, I felt a sadness rush over my body. I had brought a few images I knew I would never see again. They were the only copies of this moment in time, and I felt deeply attached to the people in the photos; for those reasons, I knew I had to bring them. We lit the fire in our cabin and we tore out the pages of journals where we had written all our deepest fears and insecurities and threw them in the fire as an offering to ending those feelings.

Next it was time for the pictures. I didn't want to do it. I didn't want to let go of the visual idea of a relationship that wasn't what I had thought it was. We had taken one photo at the first party we ever went to as a couple. We were drunk and happy. We looked beautiful. My Gemini lover was so different from me but felt like the missing piece of my puzzle for so long. My best friend. My baby daddy. My fiancé. The man I knew I'd grow old with. My for better or for worse. The source of so much laughter and immense pain. My partner in creation. My distraction from myself. I stared at the photo for twenty minutes, taking in our smiles, our eyes, remembering that moment so vividly. We had no idea what was in store for us. I could have never imagined this conclusion. I closed my eyes tightly, and I threw the one-of-one picture into the flames and watched the edges curl up and our faces turn into blobs of ash. I sobbed uncontrollably for thirty minutes. My perfect family dynamic had been over before this moment, but watching the image of it disintegrate made the ending real.

This release was not the last of my mourning or sorrow, but it was my first step in finally moving forward. I had been stuck in my pain and rage only moving a few inches toward self-discovery. The magic mushroom, paired with the element of fire, was a catalyst for my release and has been a catalyst for many more releases since then.

My intentional plant medicine ceremonies have also only further solidified my intuitive powers, which I have questioned since childhood. As a little girl, I remember seeing energy and spirits up close and personal. Yes, I saw ghosts. I was frightened by this unpredictable ability, and I told myself it wasn't real. Adults told me so, too. Eventually, these visions stopped, but my sensitivity to energy never did. Organized religion never spoke to me in the ways that the elements around me did. My connection to my gut instinct, the way my body reacts to energy, and my intuition has guided and protected me in ways I only began to understand as an adult who had finally tapped back in.

Nature has always been a place where these messages come

quickly. The ocean and moon have been my guides and my comfort. Even as I sit here writing this chapter, it was brought to my attention that today there is a full moon in Scorpio, my sun sign. It's a lunar eclipse moon, which is a sight to see if you haven't ever taken a moment to look up and see one in all its glory. Tonight's moon is a flower moon, which encourages rituals of fire and release. It's not a coincidence that I'm writing a chapter on my experience with these exact elements. This is how my life works now, because I am finally open to the messages and lessons God or Spirit lays out for me.

Now, before any Christians or others who are reading this book get uncomfortable with all this talk of the moon and stars, I want you to understand that feeling connected to the elements around you is not the same as challenging your belief in whatever god you believe in. The first people on Earth used the moon, stars, and elements to create the foundation of much of our belief systems, long before they were gentrified, whitewashed, and changed into elements of control. Do you really think the moon just sits in the sky for no reason? Or that the stars are just there to look at? Do you really think the ocean and all the elements around us were created just because? Nature is the oldest religion. Before missionaries went around spreading their truths to civilizations that already had their own, the original humans relied on what was naturally shown and given to them by their gods and goddesses. These were the ways people built their faith and practices. We could go into the history of all this, but this isn't that book. I just ask that you have an open heart and mind when reading how we have been able to find faith and trust in the process of life and existence.

This faith is what brought Milah and me together. We share a similar understanding that the trends in the stars are real and that our intuition isn't déjà vu. Yes, we're those women, the ones who will ask you your time and location of birth while ordering a chai latte, easy ice, two raw sugars, please. We're Black girls who grew up in white spaces, and it wasn't all great but it wasn't all bad either, because those white people be knowing shit: namely, what Black and brown people knew long before all this earthy shit became mainstream. In short, we are some witchy bitches—the good kind, for those who need reassurance.

Although the gifts of Mother Earth, and rituals using cannabis and mushrooms, have been a tool in my rediscovery, another modality has helped me cope with my stress and anxiety. It's the driver of this boat, if you will—the Megan Thee Stallion to my bottle of D'ussé. Podcasting has been a huge driver in my healing. Being able to talk daily with my best friend and others has helped me put the pieces of my life back together and put things in perspective for myself as a woman and mother. As I began to make space for this new person that I was birthing, I also began to understand the powers that we hold as women. My partnership with Jamilah has been a testament that when women come together, we are fucking unstoppable. We are the salt of the earth and the birthers of everything living. We are the ancient multitaskers, the empresses of checks and balances, and the visionaries of civilizations they left out of history books. We dream it, we see it, and we follow through. We are the OG manifesters.

"Manifesting" is a buzzword, thanks to social media and the thousands of experts who promise to teach you how to manifest a milli into your bank account. I can't promise that you'll manifest a million dollars in thirty days by lighting a candle and talking to yourself in the mirror every day. I can promise that you'll be on your way there if you see it, believe it, and put action and intention behind that dream of a million dollars. Often people focus on the end result when manifesting instead of also envisioning the work that will need to be done in order to make that vision come to life. Imagine dreaming and longing to have a child but not once thinking about the positive pregnancy test, the first baby bump picture, or the beautiful maternity shoot you'll surely have. You don't just skip that part. You can't, if you actually want what you are asking for.

The power of manifestation has been an incredible tool in my life over the duration of building *Good Moms Bad Choices* with Jamilah and creating the lifestyle I want to live. People talk about manifesting all the time during lunar shifts and planetary alignments. Yes, these factors can be powerful activators, but it's deeper than just wishing upon a fucking star and hoping for the best. You must believe that you can have what you are asking for. You must see it. You must talk about it as if it's already yours, even when there are moments you doubt yourself. Your actions, both physical and mental, have to support what you are inviting in. You will not manifest that million dollars if you are careless with your spending and not taking small steps daily to be ready to receive those blessings. You have also probably manifested things in your life unknowingly, because you believed you deserved whatever it was that fell into your lap. Personally, I have called in opportunities, phone calls, business deals, experiences, money, and even love.

Whether you are manifesting your dream job, your dream

relationship, or your ideal lifestyle, it's important to be very clear about what that looks like for you. My mother told me to write down a list and check it twice. Be as specific as you can, and don't be modest about your desires. You may feel that it isn't realistic to ask for a handsome, six-foot-tall man with the perfect penis and a heart of gold, and you may decide to scale back. Don't. Why would you downplay your desires and what you want? Is the reason that you feel you don't deserve what you want? Maybe you have work to do. We all do, babe. Writing your desire down, coming back to this desire daily, and believing you deserve to see it fulfilled will motivate you to start taking steps to get ready for Mr. Big Dick, if that's what you're into, to walk through your door.

We so often try to belittle our needs and wants because they seem too grandiose or selfish. Manifesting is where selfishness meets opportunity. Your wants are not selfish. You're not asking for too much. My love manifestation chart is wild. My first attempt was vague, so I got everything I asked for, which was a mediocre version of what I wanted. When I went back again and became more detailed, the lovers who came in began to reflect my list.

The "right" situation may not appear immediately. It's up to you to decide what feels designed for you and what is just a pit stop on the way to your destination. The pit stops matter, because they are confirmation that you are not asking for too much, and they keep you going until you find what feels divine.

Please Don't Wish Upon a Star

Yes, manifesting can be a wonderful tool on the full moon and all that jazz, but you don't need a star or moon in the sky to call in what you want. Below are a few simple steps to help you start manifesting right now.

In your journal, answer the following questions:

What am I manifesting?
What am I doing to make this happen?

Next, list the things you want. I always include at least four descriptors under every ask because, as my mama said, it's important to be specific and detailed.

What follows is an example of one quality I am looking for in a man and a detailed list of what that quality means. These lists get long, and they should! Go crazy.

A FAMILY-ORIENTED MAN

- has a good relationship with his mother;
- has a strong bond with his children, if he has any;
- loves my family and makes an effort to get to know them and spend time with them;
- likes to plan family vacations without me asking;
- encourages healing in both of our family dynamics where healing is needed; and
- loves my child like his own.

Go deeper with our digital "how to's" at goodmomsbadchoices .com.

Continued

Now write down what you are going to do to be ready to receive this desire that you're manifesting. List as many things as you can, and then circle three that you can start doing right now.

I also had to ask myself, What work have I done to be ready for someone like this to walk into my life? Will I be prepared? Will I be able to value him, and will I be of value to him? Can I offer him what is on his list? We often ask for relationships or situations to show up when we aren't ready to receive them, as if their existence will make us catch up. It won't. You must do the work, because that man or that situation will pass you by if you're not also prepared to show up in the ways you want your desired person or situation to show up for you. Are you ready to do the work?

Good. Because, bitch, the time is now.

MILAH

I wish I could say that after my split and one fuck, I was cured of all the pain the many transitions of my life had bestowed upon me, but there were more challenges than I could count. I felt liberated in some ways, but in many ways I still felt alone AF—incomplete and angry, actually. Although I had been figuring out a lot of things solo already, I still had this new, overwhelming sense that I had to make shit happen completely on my own. The truth was, I was now solely responsible for my wins and also my failures. If my house came crashing down, there was literally no one else there to help put it back together. In addition, I was now responsible for another human.

I had been up and down with my finances and "situations" before, but I had never been down while caring for a child. There's a huge difference between "struggling" solo and subjecting a small child to a struggle he or she never asked for. As a lone twenty-something-year-old in the world, you could crash on a friend's couch for a few weeks or go out of town for an extended period of time to avoid your problems and "find yourself." However, there is definitely a different level of "Fuck shit" you can get away with when you have a child and you are in your thirties. This reality created a huge hole of anxiety and uncertainty in my stomach. My supposed-to-be-forever, my friend, my high school sweetheart had failed me, and I was out in the world alone to figure it out. My perfect fantasy life was no longer, and it took hundreds of days of waking up alone for me to accept the reality of my decisions. Being a "single mom" was no walk in the park; there were even more challenges than when I was partnered. I felt like baby Bambi stumbling to find my footing in the world alone.

Coming to terms not only with single parenthood but also with what I needed to thrive and not just survive, I experienced a whirlwind of emotions in this phase. I simultaneously felt a sense of newfound freedom, a desire to reexplore and discover myself as a single woman, and also a deep longing to retreat back to "my family" and my comfort zone. In short, I was sad and very much feeling as though I had the entire world on my shoulders. I was an independent aesthetician struggling to find a consistent clientele and the perfectly curated Instagram marketing strategy. I was responsible for the entire rent for a two-bedroom, two-bathroom apartment in overpriced-ass LA. I was scared and desperate to figure it out without having to reenter the world of clocking in. At some point I put my extra

Affirmation

I am open to gentle lessons and to healing in all
the forms it may manifest.

bedroom on Airbnb in hopes that I'd cover at least half of my expenses. Some people (and I am some people) would say welcoming strangers into your home when you have a small child is absolutely in-fucking-sane, and in many ways they are correct. However, nothing comes between a determined mother and her destiny if she's focused enough.

I was determined not to fail. Yet I still fell short. I was struggling. Bills and rent were late pretty much every month, and I was spiraling and backstepping into my old patterns. Occasionally, I was even slipping up and back onto the dick of my baby daddy. Eventually, I was forced to move out of my apartment and move back in with my mom, until that no longer worked. My car got repoed, my world seemed to be falling apart, and I had no one I could reach out to for help. Luna was depending on me, and I could depend on no one. I was scared I would never get back on my feet. Yet somehow, I still managed to consistently produce shows weekly for *Good Moms Bad Choices*. No one but Erica knew what I was going through, because it was too painful to talk about. *Good Moms Bad Choices* felt like my only safe space. We weren't making a single dime, really, but everything in my spirit told me it was only a matter of time.

During this two-year period, it seemed my life was playing out oddly in two separate universes. On the one hand, I was displaced, staying with friends, financially struggling, and falling into a state of both depression and emergency. Most of my friends had support systems, backups if shit hit the fan—savings accounts parents had in place for them, partners and family members who could catch them if they fell. For me, that wasn't the case, which made it difficult to cope, with me feeling that my world was unfair and overwhelming. On the other hand, I knew that *Good Moms* was right where I was supposed to be, even though it was taking up a lot of time without any financial return.

I started to realize that *Good Moms* was something much deeper than just a podcast I had decided to start with a random friend. It had become my safe haven—my therapy, my community, and in some ways my savior. It had become a spiritual practice, our oral ritual. A magical covenant that spawned a divine mystic shift and brought together a collective. A way to reflect on my feelings, show up for something consistently, have purpose and practice. The power and comfort that producing the podcast provided for me went much deeper than financial security. Spirit was whispering to me, *You are protected, you are cared for, and everything is going to be okay.*

I prayed every day for a shift. Every time I caught an angel number, I took the time to manifest the shifts I wanted to see. I visualized me and Luna in our new apartment, our safety, and how it physically would feel in my spirit to feel settled. I never stopped or gave up. Looking back, I see that I was suffering, but my spirit believed and understood that what was mine was already mine, and there was nothing to truly worry about. Sure enough, I eventually moved into a new apartment with my baby.

She had her own room, and I got a car. It felt as if Spirit had finally answered my prayers—prayers that I had begun to worry were falling on deaf ears. There was a major shift taking place, and I could feel it in my soul. Sometimes you don't understand the timing; you just have to trust the direction, and that's what I did.

About a month into settling into my apartment, I got an unlikely call from a guest we had previously had on the show. As we do with most of our guests, we had hit it off with this one, so I wasn't shocked to see her name appear on my caller ID. We had laughed, cried, and connected on the show, but I hadn't really spoken to her since, apart from a text or DM here or there. She was calling to tell me about a vision she had of me during a "ceremony"; this didn't surprise me because I understood that Ariél, like many of my associates, was a good witch and a bohemian. She and her husband, Saint, were regular "burners" (people who attended the hard-core weeklong hippie festival in the desert) and free spirits.

Ariél was calling to honor her vision and ask if I'd star in a short film she was directing for a future art exhibition. The offer sounded amazing, but the shoot would take place in Mexico on Christmas Day, and I would have to be gone for a week. Not only was this call random, but it came only a few weeks after I had settled into an apartment. Ariél was asking me to spend a week with just her and her husband. I loved them, but I really had never spent more than an hour with either of them. Were they trying to invite me into some freaky international threesome that I'd be obliged to participate in for a full week?

Like many women, I couldn't make a decision on my own, so

I consulted with the board of bitches who aren't me, a.k.a. Erica.

"Girl, do you really need to be away from your kid on Christmas? Can you do it a different week?"

"No, they can't. Also it's a free trip to Mexico. And her vision saw me of all people—maybe I need to follow her vision? Do you think they are trying to do some freaky threesome shit?"

"Maybe! You know they are very free," Erica said, laughing but serious as hell.

I sat on the offer for a couple days until eventually I agreed. What the fuck did I have to lose? I was getting a free trip to Mexico for Christmas. Everyone would just have to judge me for being an absent mother during the holiday season. Hell, Luna would have a lot of other Christmases. But as expected, everyone did judge me. My BD talked major shit, called me a terrible mother for not being present on Luna's fifth Christmas, blah blah blah. Honestly, I didn't give two fucks. Spirit summoned me, and I answered the call by simply saying yes. I realized I've said yes in my life more often than most, and I'm kind of proud of my ability to take risks and just go for it when most can't. I had no idea what I was getting into or what weird shit I would be faced with once I made it to this small town in Mexico, but I figured, fuck it. I knew Ariel and Saint enough to know they weren't crazy. I'd be cared for, get compensated, and get a free trip and some dope-ass images out of it. I surrendered.

When I arrived in Mexico, I was sure I had made the right decision. After almost two years of stress, struggle, and hustle, I needed to breathe. I had been feeling in limbo and unsafe for so long that I hadn't realized how desperately I needed to ground myself. The moment I made it to this beautiful Mexican cottage off a dirt road and embraced my people, I knew I was in the right place and with the right company to guide me into a place to surrender. The driver, whom I dubbed my Mexican grandmother by the end of our hour-long drive to the house, left us, and there I was in the middle of nowhere with this hippie couple. The house was circular and quiet, with a garden, small pool, rooftop, and outdoor shower. I was exactly where I was supposed to be. Ariel and I walked to the ocean, got topless, and confided in each other. I was with my people, and it felt so good.

It dawned on me that sometimes it's necessary to just go where your heart leads you. Sometimes that's among people who haven't known you your whole life or even for very long. I believe that, in some cases, your soul knows people longer than your body has. Sometimes the people who have known you the longest and loved you the longest hold you to a version of yourself that no longer is you.

On this adventure, I didn't hold myself to any old forms; after all, I was changing, and it became clear that Ariél and Saint had been sent to help me accept my own transformation. They each gently led me to different parts of myself and showed me how to be free in my body without doing anything except being present in their own. A divine transmuting was taking place. With each day on this new and foreign land, I was changed. I was grounded.

On Christmas Day, my platonic husband and wife planned a little surprise getaway for our pseudo family to a small town called Todos Santos. To my surprise, we arrived at an even more beautiful home on the coast. This house was more modern, made of concrete and laced with multiple patios, balconies, and outdoor fireplaces. It was like a modern concrete beachside castle. Every day I was there I had to pinch myself, hardly believing how fucking cool my life had become when I said yes to me. Every little beautiful detail was a message from the universe affirming that following my intuition was always worth it. I finally felt like the main character in a princess movie. All the colors around me were vibrant. Butterflies seemed to flutter by in slow motion, and I could hear the birds singing for me. This fairy tale was real, and I wasn't locked up in any tower awaiting somebody's son to come release me. I just woke up one day and kicked the door down my damn self. I was free.

The second day at the castle, we all planned to "take a journey," which would be led by LSD. I felt I was being anointed by LSD shamans in this realm—chauffeured in and led intentionally. I hadn't really had much experience taking a "drug" as a medicine and allowing it to guide me. I was nervous, because I understood how, when you use this kind of medicine, the tangible world tends to melt away, and your mind takes you where your energy needs to flow. But someone once told me, "Don't find LSD. Let LSD find you." And I never forgot these words. So here I was, in the desert, in a concrete castle on the coast of the Pacific Ocean, with two people who absolutely felt like spirit guides.

We gathered around the couch, each said our intentions out loud, licked a small drip of tasteless liquid gold off the back of our hands, and took off—this time into the infinite universe of ourselves together. We hit the beach, and as soon as our feet hit the sand, and our faces hit the sun, we beamed with pure joy that felt infectious—as though we were small children, having the *best day ever*! Ariel and I stripped down in front of the Pacific Ocean and frolicked in and out of the water. The ocean looked laced with diamonds, sparkling for us. The waves crashed and kissed our feet like we were goddesses, and we sat at the shoreline, legs spread wide open, backs against the sand, and let her kiss our sweet little yonis.

The world was making love to us. Every single thing felt like a ball of beautiful bliss. I was falling in love with life in a way that I had never experienced before. All three of us giggled, cartwheeled, and laughed and laughed and laughed until we cried. We rolled around in the sand and twirled in and out of the crashing waves until we were dizzy and fell to our knees. We must have laughed and played for hours. We were in our own world. No, we were on our own planet, in a different universe. As the sun danced west, we looked around, and suddenly, to our surprise, we saw that there were actually other people on this beach—lots of other people, in fact, all in proper beach attire.

We had been so consumed by our joy that it hadn't dawned on us how bizarre we must've looked, naked and frolicking like children on this nonnude beach all day. Then Saint said to us, "Girls, you do know there are families and children here?" It was as though Ariel and I took off the blinders of our world and peered into the world of the mortals, where we were surrounded by fully clothed families and random passersby. This realization might have embarrassed some people. But not us—we roared with even more laughter. How the fuck had we been out here all day and literally hadn't noticed or acknowledged a single human? The reason was that we were having a cosmic experience—a rare meeting of worlds where others and their opinions didn't exist. When reality began to settle in, we still weren't ashamed of our naked bodies; instead, everyone else seemed out of place. Neither of us could manage to figure out how to put our bikinis back on, so we put on sunglasses and hats instead and giggled our naked little butts back up to our castle.

We migrated to another balcony on the second floor, where we turned on the fireplace and began our nightly ritual of a dance party. I felt the journey coming to an end. We unintentionally gathered in a circle underneath the beaming moon and night sky, still naked but with blankets. As Ariel scrolled through a few songs on her playlist, a woman's voice began to sing a poem. Immediately my spirit noticed the song. I could make out some of the words of the poem, but not really; I could just tell she was speaking to women. As the women's prayer continued to play, I felt an odd pulling of my heartstrings. Don't get me wrong, I'm a sensitive Cancer, but hearing a random song that was new to me had never made me feel emotional. But for some reason, on this evening, in a kumbaya circle, I felt a need to express emotion when I heard this woman's voice sing this song. Under any other circumstance I would have never felt comfortable submitting to these emotions, but with these two people I allowed my body to openly express whatever it needed to express. I felt tears slowly begin to roll down my face.

Internally, I was still having a conversation with myself: *What is happening? Why am I crying?* I didn't have the answer, but I let things out anyway. The tears continued, heavier and heavier. I felt myself begin to take deep gut breaths. But I wasn't trying to regulate or contain my emotions as I would normally with breath; I was breathing to release something. My breathing became deeper with each inhale. I was bawling, crying uncontrollably, and my exhales transmuted into sounds: deep, primal grunts from the pits of my belly and my womb. I couldn't stop. The grunts turned into growls, then those primal growls transmuted into howls, until I was crying and screaming. The last conscious thought I had was that someone was going to call the police, and then I slipped into the universe.

I was now screaming and crying at the top of my lungs, and there was nothing I could do to stop it. I was grounded on the floor on my knees, chest and face facing the moon, when I started to feel female energy that wasn't my own. Some kind of spiritual technology was unlocking in my body. From my gut and womb and chest, pure female energy came through, but it wasn't my own. Somehow I knew it was the energy of the women in my family. This was the first time I had ever experienced my body channeling my female ancestors, or any ancestors for that matter. With each scream, I could feel their pain passing through my chest and exiting through my mouth. I had a foreign feeling of opening hidden doors and pockets inside my soul and releasing pain I hadn't even known was there. I felt my mother's pain, my grandmother's pain, and the pain of women in my family I had never met; in that moment, I knew them and understood them, and they understood me. I purged with voice until I combusted. I felt like a ball of fire in the universe, burning hot at light speeds through darkness. I felt I had exploded from the inside out and rebirthed myself. After every sound in my body had been released and I literally could not produce another, I collapsed to the ground, weeping.

Had I just had a "soul-to-soul" encounter with all the women who had created me? I was in disbelief. After this release, I felt the same feeling I felt when they placed Luna on my chest after I had chauffeured her earth-side through the ether. I sobbed on the ground, and Saint and Ariél covered me with their arms and hands as though I was a baby in a cocoon.

I had no words to describe what the fuck I had just experienced, and I didn't need any. Ariel and Saint witnessed, ushered, and held me through this deeply healing experience. When I finally managed to lift my head from the cement, they grounded me by embracing me while I wept. I felt protective father energy, nurturing guided mother energy, and even an intimate romantic love and security. In those moments, my conscious mind understood that the lines of intimacy, security, and love were nonexistent. Life was made of watercolor, and love bled into every single crevasse if we allowed it to. At that time, there were no two souls I was closer to—didn't matter if they were white or hippies, or young or old, or male or female. When they embraced me together during and after that experience, I felt that we were one. I was safe and free at the same time, and it was priceless and unforgettable. They were souls who had protected and guided and loved me a million times before; any sense of separation I had ever felt from anyone different from me wasn't real. I tapped into a spiritual well inside of myself and entered into a paradigm in which I controlled the narrative.

I had really experienced my own power during that journey, and there was no going back. That I was activated was an understatement. I had touched magic, and I'm not even talking about the LSD. The LSD was a vessel to remove the limits of my mind and usher me into the spirit realm. The spirit realm was the reality; everything else was made up. The rest of my trip was absolute bliss. I left Ariel and Saint to meet some of my friends and a new lover, and I was on fire to share what I had discovered with anyone and everyone who would moan with me and listen.

To my reader, I want to be clear that I am not advising you to lose all sense of responsibility and to go get fucked up or high. I am, however, encouraging you to be open to the mystical possibilities of life. Be intentional about tapping into your childlike self and tending to that inner child. I'm urging you to take your pleasure and need for fun and adventure as seriously as you take your marriages and kids. Watering your pleasure nurses and feeds the garden that often nourishes the people we love.

Whatever it looks like for you, step outside of the role of parent, adult, and authority, and do silly shit. For me, it took a leap of faith, intentionally stepping into an alternate realm using LSD as my coach of choice. Your coach may look completely different. Your plant medicine may be simply setting an intention over a hot cup of cacao (another plant medicine)—or, hell, even a cup of water (water molecules mutate with energy). We all "undress" differently, and Spirit always brings messages and lessons to each us differently. Be open to receiving them, whether these messages are presented in the form of a spontaneous adventure, a women's retreat, or a magic mushroom. Outside of your comfort zone is where change happens.

CHAPTER 9

FIND
Your Tribe

We all know that making friends in adulthood can be difficult—really difficult. However, we have personally experienced the power of sisterhood. Women need women. In order to find your tribe, you have to be open, meaning that you have to court your friends and treat platonic friendships just as you would treat romantic ones. Women together are more powerful than women alone.

ERICA

Jamilah is my platonic wife. Yes, you heard me correctly: my platonic wife. This term seems to ruffle men's feathers, and for that very reason I make sure to use it every chance I get. Words matter to this society we live in, but for me, the intention behind these labels we've created matters so much more. What is the duty of a wife, anyway? Well, that's a very layered question in the world we live in. The basics are to love and protect your partner, to support them through the different versions of themselves, respect them, hold space where they lack, nurture them, listen to them, be honest when they are fucking up, and advocate for their happiness as if it's yours. Jamilah does all these things for me, and I hope I do

Affirmation

I trust women. I trust that they can and will show up for me.

the same for her. We do many of the things a husband and wife do, but without the intimacy of sex. Our daughters are on the same soccer team, we take vacations together with the kids and without, we share bank accounts, we cry together, we talk about our plans for the future, and we even buy land together.

We are often fed this idea in modern-day society that "soulmate" and "life partner" are titles reserved for romantic partners. If you believe in past lives, then it would be easy to believe that a lover from another lifetime can show up in this one as your closest friend or even your parent. There is a cosmic connection Jamilah and I embody when we're together, and I believe that we have known each other in other realms. The way the deepness and richness of our friendship comes naturally tells me so. I know that it was no mistake that I felt an unfamiliar calling to get off my ass, drop the baby off, and make friends with a stranger that night.

For me, desperation and saying yes were the first steps in shifting toward a new life and friendship. Let this be a sign that if you feel stuck and your spirit is calling you to do something different or maybe even drastic, do it. Be responsible-ish, but do that shit. Take a risk and get uncomfortable. You may be surprised how stepping outside of your regular routine can help change the trajectory of your life. I know that it did for me, just as it does in every rom-com I have ever loved. Sitting down every week to record a podcast with a semistranger was the best

risk I ever took. If you listen to the first episode of our podcast—
"Sex, Apps, and Kids"—you can hear the newness of our friendship. I didn't even know she went by Milah until after the first
fifteen seconds of this episode.

Over the past five years, we have truly cultivated a bond, on
and off the mic, that I treasure and work hard to keep healthy.
Just in case you didn't know, friendships also require work,
prayer, and radical honesty. As women, we work overtime trying
to save romantic relationships. Imagine putting that energy into
your friendships with women. Imagine taking the faith you have
in all these unhealed men and lovers and placing it instead in the
girl at work who you think doesn't like you but who, in reality,
just battles with social anxiety. We give lust and love the benefit
of the doubt, but not our sisters. We have to stop this madness.

I can hear you saying, "So you mean to tell me all I have to
do is take a chance and meet a stranger at a bar, and I'll meet
the Jamilah to my Erica?" Maybe, but probably not. All of our
destinies are different. Making friends as adults is hard. People already have their circles and cliques, and trying to insert
yourself into their established tribe feels pushy. You must be
bolder and a little more strategic as you get older when you
find that you want to change or begin your tribe. And if, as
you are reading this, the idea of making female friends triggers
negative thoughts—*Every woman I meet betrays me*, maybe, or
Female friends can't be trusted—I need you to look within yourself and ask yourself a series of very honest and hard questions,
remembering that you yourself are the common denominator in
cyclical, negative encounters and relationships.

So here it goes: First, when did you decide you can't trust

women? What is your biggest fear when making a new friend? What are you looking for in a friendship? What do you need to feel safe in a friendship? What is one way you may play a part in your distrust or difficulty in making friends?

What I have found through my years of talking to women who in some ways idealize the friendship Jamilah and I have is that many fear making new friends because they were betrayed in the past. Whether these wrongdoings happened in childhood or involved a partner, women with these triggers are looking for friendships to fill voids or to prove that the outcome will be different this time. This approach will set your friendships up for disaster. People will always disappoint you if you put them to a test they don't even know they're taking. For example, if I have a fear that people will not follow through on plans after they are made, and I make plans with a new co-worker whose vibe I like, but she cancels day of, I will be disappointed and think that she doesn't care about hanging out with me—when the real story is that she mismanaged her calendar and couldn't get someone to watch her son but chose not to share those details with me.

Taking things personally will have you on your own island, alone, blaming everyone for your solitude. To be blunt, it's easier to be the victim than to ask yourself what role you've played in creating your isolation or distrust of platonic connection. If you want a different result in any relationship, it is crucial that you dig deep, check your traumas, and work diligently on pinpointing your triggers as they happen. In this scenario, instead of accepting the co-worker's cancellation without knowing the reason, you could ask a follow-up question, such as "I was looking forward to hanging out, is everything okay? Is there any way I can help?" This would allow your friend suitor to feel supported and share why she is canceling, in turn giving you solace in knowing that the cancellation wasn't personal.

Because guess what, babe?—you do need the Erica to your Jamilah, and female friendships do fucking matter. The best male friend you could have will still never share with you women's universal experience as vagina holders. Women in your life may have done you wrong, but so have men, and somehow you still hold space for them. We must give women the same grace, if not more! We have been pitted against one another since men figured out how divinely powerful we are together. Seriously, if women ran the world, things would look pretty different. But we can't change history. All we can do is try our best to change the trajectory of our own stories about friendships, sisterhood, and trust.

I'll be honest, I wasn't always a girl's girl. I had girlfriends, but I valued attention from boys and men more than the validation I received from my closest girlfriends. Chalk it up to those daddy issues we talked about a few chapters back or to what my mother told me more than once when I was a young girl navigating schoolyard drama—that if a girl didn't like me or wasn't nice to me, she was just jealous. Maybe sometimes Mom was right, but this advice deepened my distrust for girls and set my competitive spirit up for many years of feeling challenged by other girls similar to me instead of trying to be close to them because of our similarities. I wanted to be the only alpha in the group—the one who called the shots or shifted the energy. Anyone else who could do that threatened my confidence and sense of my own value. I wish I could pinpoint exactly when this belief shifted for me, but I think it was a slow transition as I met other alpha women who showed up for me in surprising ways.

I also believe having a daughter was a major eye-opener. When I was pregnant, I had my first Reiki session, and the main takeaway I was given was that my energy leaned heavily on the masculine. I hadn't found out the sex of my child yet, but something in my soul told me I was going to have a girl. During my session the practitioner asked me if I knew the sex. I answered no; I wasn't confident in my intuition yet.

"You are having a girl," the practitioner told me. "You have a lot of energy leaning into the masculine. She is going to help you find balance and tap in to your feminine. She is going to heal those wounds for you."

I didn't realize I had wounds at the time, but she was so right. After I had my daughter, the women who showed up for me began building that faith I hadn't known I needed. My mother, my grandmother, and the woman who helped raise me swooped in and covered me with love and support. My girlfriends who stuck with me through pregnancy checked in and comforted me the best they knew how. I began to realize I needed more mothers around me who understood what was happening to me. Hence, my encounter with Jamilah, which unlocked a newfound safety and trust in women. For some reason, that day at her daughter's birthday party, I felt inclined to share that I was both mommying and having threesomes, which in turn made Jamilah feel safe to share more intimate details of her relationship with her child's father, which she hadn't told me before.

It was through more and more honest exchanges like these that Jamilah and I became more than just friends; we became

confidants, sisters, or—if you want to piss off the men—
platonic wives. She became a mirror for me. Seeing certain
parts of her awakened the old me to come alive again. Certain
parts of her were uncomfortable for me to accept, and I had to
ask myself, *Why?* I saw in her pieces of myself that never fully
flourished, that I had suppressed or was ashamed or scared to
express. She was comfortable with her body—like, completely
comfortable. If you know Milah, her tits fight clothing, and
the tits always win. As someone who struggled with body issues, I found this triggering. I was jealous—of course she was
comfortable, she was ninety-five pounds. But her confidence
doesn't come from her size; it comes from her innate nature
to love her form no matter what size it is. Realizing that has
helped me accept my body in any shape or season. Jamilah
didn't hide her cannabis consumption from Luna and didn't
have hard rules around when her daughter could meet someone she's interested in. She danced like nobody was watching,
and she was immensely forgiving. All of these qualities helped
shape and change my perspective on how I want to show up
for myself and my daughter.

Our friendship saved my life. It brought me to my tribe—
not just the beautiful women and mothers I know day-to-day
in my life (shout out to our group text, "Tribe Chat"), but also
the millions I've engaged with over the years because of this
safe space we have created online with *Good Moms Bad Choices*.
I have spilled my guts to strangers in our DMs, and they have
done the same. For some reason, I know I'm safe with them,
which is a huge jump for me from being a young girl who
thought everything was a competition. Our community on the

Discord app is filled with thousands of women who are sharing vulnerable and funny stories, empowering one another, and meeting up in their cities to find their new besties. Our community pushed us to create an intimate space where we could put into practice all we preach, which has manifested into The Good Vibe Retreat, where we host wellness international retreats for women seeking self-care, healing, and sisterhood.

One thing I've learned from leading retreats in person is that women need permission. Women need to see other women cry so that they can cry. They need to see other women take their tops off at the pool so they can do the same. Black women need to see other Black women doing "white people shit" so they feel safe doing the same. I needed to see Jamilah be unabashedly free so that I could follow suit. This is the reason it is so important for women to have safe spaces to come together—for us to honor one another and have one another to lean on in a world that has told us we come second. It is of great urgency, especially in this time we are in now, when the patriarchy is exposed, that we smash these walls we've built up as though our lives depend on it, so that we can create the village and communities that our souls so desperately need, that the world undoubtedly is starving for, and that our ancestors intended for us to have.

If you don't already have a tribe, a best friend, or the makings of one, don't worry. It's never too late. One way to start is by tapping into our community at *Good Moms Bad Choices*. These beautiful women represent all walks of life, races, and ages, because motherhood and womanhood are not one-size-fits-all.

Love Letter to Your Bestie

Take a piece of paper and write your best friend or future bestie a love letter. Tell her why you adore her and your favorite qualities about her. Don't hold back! If you are writing this to someone you already know, I want you to mail her the letter. She deserves to feel special and to know exactly how you feel. You can encourage her to write a letter back, or not. This exercise is more for you to normalize sharing your feelings with someone you care deeply for.

If you are writing this to your future friend, I want you to include the qualities of the friendship that you are manifesting. Be detailed, as if she's already here, showing up for you. Keep this letter in a safe place.

MILAH

For the collective healing of women and the world, we must trust and empower other women so that we may trust and empower ourselves.

When I returned to the States from my time with Ariél and Saint in Mexico, I felt illuminated with magic and motivated with possibilities. It was as if I had unlocked the door to a storybook world I had not ventured to since childhood and now had the key to existing in a real-life fairy tale I looked for signs in every conversation, situation, and new friendship. I was hyperaware of how sweet every little thing was. Things went wrong, as they always do, but I began to perceive "no" as a word of protection and to understand that everything and everybody meant for me in my world would find me. As I trusted in the alignment of my life, everything became aligned.

I really started to see our podcast as a magical vessel. Through this ancient ritual of storytelling and truth, people were coming together—and not just any people, but people who were also living in their truth. All that honesty attracted other good moms who were also showing up in honesty as they were, without the burden of having to wear a mask.

My friendship with Erica has a basis in "Fuck it." Fuck it, I'm going to be honest; fuck it, I'm going to be me; just fuck it. After you've let go of a long-term partner you thought you would never lose, after you've suffered from amnesia about who you are, it's rather easy to lead with the "Fuck it, I have nothing to lose" mentality. Erica and I were so brutally honest that day at the birthday party because we had both given so much in our relationships, to our partners and families, only to watch it slip away and create huge waves of change. We had nothing else to lose and everything to gain from showing up as our authentic selves. Withstanding that shit made us somewhat fearless and definitely much stronger. When you lose yourself and then find yourself again, you will do almost anything to never end up in the same predicament; showing up as yourself seems like the only option. Our failed relationships forced us to say "Fuck the fear"; as soon as Erica decided to show up guns blazing and share her hot couple confession with me, I immediately felt safe to do the same. Honesty is medicine.

Once we decided to take that same energy and apply it to our new hobby, the fire started. It was as if truth was the secret potion that ignited the success of our friendship and our podcast. You see, honesty is not only contagious but also liberating, and it emanates some sort of gravitational pull. As humans, we aren't intended to hide from one another or from ourselves. Unfortunately, we exist in a world that has brainwashed us into believing that we must fit into a limited prototype of some sort, urging us to bend and hide in order to fit the status quo. When you hide from others, you hide from yourself. In nature, birds and trees simply exist, without the pressure of impressing the sky or the squirrels; they have the freedom to not subscribe to make-believe realities, to not stress about judgment or acceptance. We humans, the "superior species," have had a difficult time doing away with these detrimental social constructs and rules.

When we begin to dissolve the expectation of showing up as digestible versions of ourselves for everyone else, natural law conspires in our favor. When Erica and I showed up as ourselves with each other and then made the conscious decision to show up as ourselves to a virtual audience, our message disseminated effortlessly. Everything conspired for our success. It did not matter how "outrageous" or "explicit," how "wild and crazy," our topics on the podcast were; because we were honest, the shows resonated. People near and far were attracted to the brutal honesty, because we all are seeking truth in one form or another. In the first year of our podcast, we were navigating an interesting dynamic: we had committed to something big together but were still getting to know one another. Still, we shared a trust and closeness from the beginning.

A couple months after we started *Good Moms Bad Choices*, we traveled to New York after making a shot at connecting with one of the most popular Black-female-led podcasts at the time. We hadn't expected a response, but to our surprise one of the two hosts agreed to come on our show. Erica and I traveled separately to the East Coast, both of us with our kids in tow. I had just turned thirty and was dating a hot young guy on the East Coast—I called him Young Bae—so I was feeling renewed and motivated in my new space as a podcaster and a single woman.

While I was away for my thirtieth birthday, I started to notice my breasts becoming sensitive and enlarged, and my period was late. I ignored these signs, because I figured God wasn't asshole enough to let me become pregnant just as I reached the threshold of grown-woman status. But apparently God didn't care about being popular with me. Hours before I took a train and a subway in ninety-degree muggy heat from New Jersey to Manhattan, I took a pregnancy test that came out positive. I was shooketh. But I had to get my shit together and make it to our big interview on time.

I arrived to the hotel tardy and nervous but ready to chat. We put headphones on our kids and pushed the record button, but right before we pushed it, Erica offered me tequila from the mini bar. I declined, causing both her and this guest and stranger I had just met to raise their eyebrows. I discovered that day that being an "active podcaster" meant never biting your tongue—like, *never*. Our new acquaintance said, "Why, bitch, are you pregnant?" Damn, I hadn't even been able to tell Erica yet. Despite my reluctance, I was on the spot. Erica was already aware my period was late, so both of them gave me blank stares, and being the honest bitch I am, I confessed my new news.

"Yeah, I just took a test."

"Are you going to keep it?" the guest asked. It was my turn for a blank stare. I honestly hadn't processed the information yet, and I was terrified of my new friend and podcast mate judging me. Erica must've felt my energy, because she brushed off the question and said, "We can talk later." We continued to record the episode, "Raw Sex, Strange Sex, Paid Sex," which turned out to be a great episode, even though our kids were in the room so we had to periodically pause our recording. As always, we were brutally honest, and so we all felt like besties by the time the two-hour recording was over—at least, so I thought.

I later had a one-on-one conversation with Erica about the pickle I had found myself in. I felt dumb, ashamed, and embarrassed. I had barely even started dating Young Bae exclusively, and this was not what I wanted. Erica was 200 percent a friend and not a business partner to me when conversing about this incredibly sensitive topic. I had never been pregnant since my "live birth" (the medical term they use at clinics for a pregnancy carried to term). Considering having an abortion felt completely different than it did in high school or even college. The guilt that polluted my body when I thought about terminating the pregnancy was completely different from how I felt when I hadn't already experienced a full-term pregnancy and birth. To my surprise, Erica never brought up the business side of this decision, even after I brought it up as a concern. The guy I was casually seeing decided he really wanted me to see the pregnancy through—and not only that, but he suddenly also wanted us "to be together."

"You have to weigh the options," Erica told me compassionately. "Do you see yourself moving to New Jersey?"

I didn't. However, I was still kind of fresh out of my BD relationship and felt my heart tug at the thought of someone choosing me and of being semistable financially. It's crazy how the thing you're deprived of, when it presents itself even to a slight degree in the next person, suddenly looks like an oasis in a dry desert. Young Bae was younger than me but had a steady union job, and at the time the thought of stability warmed my heart. I went back and forth about the possibilities. I sought my friends' opinions. All of them—except Erica—advised me, "Fuck, no!" I leaned in, and Erica continually covered me in loving words and real-life scenarios.

Meanwhile, the guy prematurely informed his friends and family without my consent and consistently tried to convince me that relocating and leaving behind my "hobby," a.k.a. the podcast, was well worth it. I was confused, to say the least, but everything in my gut told me no. The parts of me that wanted to go with Young Bae's plans for us were the parts of me attached deeply to fear and the mindset of scarcity. Finally, I decided for the first time that safety and people-pleasing weren't going to rule me. After telling

Young Bae I would have his baby, I reconsidered and reneged. It was for the best; his disrespect, disdain for women, and jealousy began to reveal themselves, and I had just come out of an emotional prison with a person with similar qualities.

It was 5 a.m., still dark out, when Erica called me to come outside my house. I had stayed up all night contemplating whether I was making a bad choice, and I had already dragged my feet way too long on this, so long I knew that the seed growing inside me was going to be a boy. I was crushed. I got in the passenger side of Erica's car while Irie slept in the back seat. I was ashamed and feeling that I was already terrible at being in my thirties. We sat in silence for a while, until Erica asked, "Are you okay?"

"Yeah," I said without hesitation.

"It's okay if you're not okay, Milah."

I don't know why, but her comment made the lump in my throat grow. I wasn't okay. I was suppressing again—attempting to be strong and just get through it—but Erica could feel my energy despite what I was trying to convey. She reached over from the driver's seat and grabbed my hand at a red light, and I silently let the tears roll down my face. I was tired of my bad choices, even if I was on the way to making a good choice.

In that moment, I felt our friendship solidify. It had been so long since anyone, including myself, had actually asked how I was feeling. She walked me inside the clinic even though I had told her not to worry, I could go in solo. She waited until I was called and silently held space for me in a way I didn't know I needed. That was the morning I began to fall platonically in love with Erica. There was never a moment she bashed me or judged me; she just sat next to me while I came to my own conclusion, no matter what that was. After the procedure, I immediately felt lighter. I knew I had made the right choice. I knew my life wasn't meant to be lived as a young New Jersey housewife navigating two jealous baby daddies on separate coasts. You see, we all make mistakes. We are all human; mistakes don't make us terrible people. In fact, even bad choices always come with good lessons attached to them. Sometimes you make bad choices a lot of times, and that's okay, too. We take time to learn, just as children do.

Weeks afterward, Erica and I reunited with the New York podcaster who had been our guest, along with a man who was another popular fellow podcaster. It was our first time meeting him, and we really wanted him to come on our show. We all met for dinner, and within five minutes of us sitting down, our New York podcast associate urged me to tell the story about "that time you got paid for sex." I was frozen but tried to brush it off with laughter. Granted, I had told the story during our episode; I felt she was being a bit facetious and putting me on the spot, but I giggled it off and told my story. Maybe this is how podcasters were? By the time the night ended, I had forgotten all about it. We hit it off with our new friend, exchanged info, and made an agreement to keep in touch. A few weeks later, he asked me whether I was pregnant. Confused AF, I responded no, and then it dawned on me that our "friend," the New York podcaster, was also a rat. After realizing this, I told the other podcaster, "I was pregnant, but I'm not anymore." "*Why? Who told you that?*" But I already knew the answer.

Rule number one in finding your tribe: everybody ain't your tribe. I was hurt by this discovery but, honestly, not surprised. It was one of my first lessons about two things: (1) trusting everybody and anybody is not a good idea; and (2) all girls aren't "girl's girls," and they aren't automatically going to keep your secrets or have your back. I'm glad, though, that I didn't allow that one experience to cause me to lose all hope and trust in women or in new friendships. Truth is, some people won't be kind to you or respond in kind to your honesty. Some may even put on and pretend to be cool and loyal. But that doesn't mean you have to change how you interact with all people or shut down all possibilities of new friendships. I know how hard it can be making friends as an adult. It isn't junior high, where you can scope out and target new friends in a classroom or auditorium and then ask to sit with them at lunch or during an assembly. We don't have to stop trusting people or seeking out real friends in our adult lives, though. It's simply the nature of the game: some apples are just sour, hating-ass apples, and you need to just leave their rotten asses right where you found them.

Thankfully, I felt more empowered in my new connection with Erica than I felt disconnected from women overall. There was purpose in the women and people I was meeting through *Good Moms*, even the bitch who told a stranger I was pregnant for absolutely no reason at all except to be a hater. Every single human I sat down with left me with a little gem—some little piece of knowledge that would shape me and never leave me, just as Ariél came to *Good Moms* and then brought me Saint and Mexico. The treasures of this robust garden fed my spirit and spread everywhere. We each had a major role to play in this movement called the quest for true life—not the programmed, unfulfilling life that we are told we deserve, but instead a life of fulfillment, fun, connection, learning, growing, healing, and positive change.

My friendship with Erica blossomed from us spending hours and hours just talking to each other and even more hours figuring shit out and fighting for something we both loved. Our commitment to our love changed me. I had never had a friend love me so intentionally. We had a lot on the line, but even more important, we had a friendship we valued, and it began to develop into a support system and little family. After-school outings, holidays, and vacations were scheduled together and with the kids. Our kids saw us build tirelessly and respected the hustle. We had been through a number of traumatic experiences side by side, and we loved and supported one another through and through.

There was nothing Erica could tell me that could make me not love and accept her, and vice versa. Even when the most uncomfortable feelings emerged, we talked about them. We were brutally honest with each other:

* "I think your new boyfriend might be a con artist."
* "I don't think he's the one, boo."
* "I'm scared you're going to abandon me and pursue your other career."
* "I'm scared I'm not enough in our business and in our friendship."
* "I'm jealous, you're so funny and witty—are you the star of the show?"

You name it, we said that shit. We said the things, we cleared the air, we apologized, we cried, we laughed, and we always loved each other. We both understood early on that our love and friendship were priceless, and we were both willing to go to great lengths to remind each other that everything between us was always in love. That understanding led us to pour that same love and energy into basically every guest we shared with and every venture we birthed. The more we became aware of the fact that our friendship was actually a divine entity, the more we prayed over it, and to this day we ask Spirit to protect our entity often. The same enlightenment and entity has led us to manifest our friendship and community in tangible form through hosting retreats on sacred international lands and has called our tribe to gather from all around the globe to experience the magic of authentic connection on a journey we call The Good Vibe Retreat.

CHAPTER 10

MOTHERHOOD
Is the Shit

Motherhood can be triggering; it also can be a catalyst to change everything in your life. For us, motherhood saved our lives. Our children are the reason we are the way we are. We wouldn't be good moms who make bad choices without our kids. Without them, we wouldn't be here telling all of our business to the world, challenging toxic motherhood stereotypes, and empowering other women like us to rewrite their own stories.

ERICA

It's true that I never wanted to be a mom. But now, eight years later, I'm that mom who takes my daughter and her friends on vacation alone. I'm the woman on the plane who will gladly sit next to your crying baby and help you shut her the hell up, because I know how stressful that can be. I still don't love to play, but seeing my daughter's face light up at the chance to hang out with me supersedes that feeling—that, and smoking a joint before we start.

Irie reminds me that staying childlike is one of the pillars of my happiness. Being a mom, I have learned to stop and really be present, because this shit really does fly by. That is one definite universal truth about parenthood. Irie's rapid evolution has forced me to practice the skill of being present. I am a futurist of sorts, and this is one of my superpowers—always striving for something more and seeing the beauty in improvement and change. But as a mother, this superpower hasn't always served her, and I've had to continue to work to become more skilled at being right here, right now.

I've had a few rude awakenings about my shortcomings when it comes to being present. Yes, seeing your child physically and rapidly change in front of you is a big reminder to live in the present, but a bigger reminder came when my daughter was able to express how she was feeling. She was around five, and I had been on autopilot for months, recording weekly episodes for *GMBC*, editing our audio and video, managing our social content, emailing brands like a psycho trying to show them that we deserved their money, all while also working another full-time job at my family business. Whenever I had a moment of time to myself, I wanted to either drink, smoke, or do something else that didn't require my mental energy.

Because most of what I do can be accomplished from my phone, in the eyes of a child it would appear that Mommy lived on that phone. Mommy did. I knew that I had been shortchanging certain parts of my role as a mother, but I felt I was doing so for the sake of our future. How was I supposed to start a successful business that required my full attention and also watch *Miraculous: Tales of*

Lady Bug & Cat Noir with my daughter? I kept putting her off and putting her needs aside. I secretly hoped that maybe she didn't notice because she played all day at school and was surrounded by love and my affection at night. But she did notice.

One evening, I had already had a long day, and my patience was low. Honestly, it had been low for weeks. I had met all her normal requests to play, have snacks, and do all the other things a child demands daily with dismissive energy, because her requests did not seem as important as what I was trying to accomplish. That night, as I tucked her into bed and went to leave her room, she asked me to lie down with her for a while. I said, "Not tonight," and kissed her; I hadn't finished work, and I just wanted to get things done. Just as I closed the door, I could hear her begin to sob. Something in me knew this was not just another bedtime meltdown. I came back and asked her what was wrong, but she wouldn't tell me. She just kept sobbing.

I began to ask her questions: "Are you just tired?"

She shook her head no.

"Are you upset about something?"

She nodded.

"Did I do something?"

She cried more.

The next question I was scared to ask because I knew the answer: "Do you feel like Mommy hasn't been paying enough attention to you?"

She nodded and turned around and put her head in her pillow.

I felt gutted. I was doing so much hard work for this person; how could I have made her feel so unseen and unimportant? I sat on the bed and had one of the realest conversations I've ever had with a five-year-old before. She told me that I always said no and that I was always on my phone. She held me accountable, and she was right. As my grown ass sat on the top of her bunk bed, I told her that Mommy had fucked up—that I had been so focused on trying improve our life that I hadn't been doing what I was supposed to. I cried and I let her see the tears run down my face. I looked her in her little eyes and apologized again and again because I needed her to understand what a real apology looks like—something I didn't get many of as a child, and never accompanied by genuine emotion. She forgave me, and we lay down together until she fell asleep.

That evening, I received a huge first-time parent reminder about the reality that kids and their basic needs don't always align with an adult's needs and wants. Here I was, tirelessly working to show her that dreams can come true through hard work and dedication, when all she really needed was my love and attention—for me to be present with her.

I vowed to create more space in my overwhelming schedule and to have better boundaries for work. Has everything been perfect since that night? No. Did I suddenly become an expert at balancing my work and home life? No. Did I never say no to my daughter again? Hell no. But I did listen to her, and I have tried and am still always trying my best to give her what she needs to be heard and supported. If you are a mother, especially a single mother, then you know that finding balance is incredibly hard once you have a little person looking for you to be the main source of attention and entertainment.

> I'm only as old as a mother as my daughter is a child, and just as she goes through growing pains, so do I.

Basically, we don't know what we don't know. It's important for our children to see us be vulnerable, fuck up, experience pain and failure; seeing us be less than perfect helps humanize us for our children. We often hear people talk about their parents as "superheroes." But then we hear how these superheroes, more often than not, cannot maintain their super status and end up disappointing their children. Or we find that we bring these superhero ideals into relationships and judge our partners for not being like our parents. This pattern is especially noticeable with men and their mothers. All their lives, their moms fought hard to put up this facade that they could handle it all, when they were really breaking down inside. Then these boys become men who expect their wives to do the same, and when we don't, they shame us.

What if, instead, we were just honest? What if we just stopped worrying about putting fear into our children and instead looked at being vulnerable as a gift? What if we showed little boys and little girls that Mommy doesn't always have it all together—that in fact she's having a hard time? Crying in front of your child is not weak. Being honest about why you've made certain decisions is not too much. Many parents maneuver through child-rearing by compartmentalizing their emotions and decision-making, because they feel that's "grown folks' business" or that their children won't respect them or will be filled with fear if parents show their vulnerability. We insult our children's intelligence by hiding or lying about why we feel or do what we do. We essentially teach them how to lie and suppress by making the obvious look like something else. Yes, you should share what needs to be shared in an age-appropriate manner, but let's stop lying to our kids, guys. They deserve the truth so that they can better understand why Mommy is overworked and underperforming in her role as parent.

Just as we need to be real about our emotions with our children, we also need to be real about sexuality and shame. We are sexual beings. Our children will inevitably have sex, and hopefully they will be better prepared than we were. I, for one, hope that my daughter doesn't choose to lose her virginity in a toolshed with some shitty teenager who doesn't really care about her or her feelings. Rewriting my personal history when it comes to how my child understands the beauty and function of her body is important to me.

Calling vaginas and penises "pee-pees" and reprimanding children the first time we witness them exploring their bodies are some of the first ways we build a harmful facade. Does it make sense to tell our children to call their body parts by pet names or euphemisms, only to have kids discover when they go to school that these aren't the names for these parts? Does it make sense to tell our children that exploring their own bodies is shameful and that they must wait until they are of an appropriate age for someone else to explore their body for them? I knew that with my child, I was going to change these conversations. It has for sure been uncomfortable and often difficult to find the right words, but the reward is so much greater. I was proud the first time I heard my daughter casually refer to her body parts by their actual names. It may sound weird, but to me that's one of the coolest parts of motherhood—watching the intentional pattern-breaking play out in the life of my child.

I hope you, too, get excited at the chance to make uncomfortable things normal for your children and realize what a privilege it is to do so.

You're creating your own version of parenthood; you can really think about some of the ways you were raised that did or didn't serve you and how you will adopt or discard those principles. Did your single mom hide from you the fact that she was dating? How did that make you feel in the long run? Did your parents smoke weed and then ridicule you the moment they found out you were exploring? Did your parent never talk to you about your body and that it was made for your pleasure and not just the pleasure of others? How would your responses and choices in life have been different if your parents had just told you the truth? My hope is that my honesty with my daughter encourages her to be honest with me—that she will come to me instead of asking smelly teenagers about sex, drugs, or any other taboo topics that we willfully ignore so we don't feel uncomfortable.

I believe that our children choose us. This is a hard pill to swallow for those children whose parents didn't do their job. Even in those circumstances, I still believe this to be true. Not everyone's incarnation in each lifetime will be pleasant. Sometimes your existence is meant to teach the person you were in your past life some very difficult lessons and challenge your

The Things We Ain't No More

In your journal, reflect on some of things that you'd like to change when it comes to being honest with your child and preparing for the inevitable influx of information your child will receive out in the world about sex, relationships, love, family dynamics, drugs, religion, history, race, and any other subjects that feel uncomfortable. How were you introduced to these topics? How do you plan to introduce them to your child? For me, it has been extremely helpful to write these things down and then have a practice conversation out loud. I'm not good at off-the-cuff, unrehearsed conversations; I have to literally talk out loud and practice what I will say so that I can figure out what feels good and doesn't. Record yourself, and play the recording back. Adjust what you say, and try again. You got this, mama!

mental and physical capacity to find the silver lining—because there is always a silver lining, I promise. Irie's entrance into the world saved me from whatever the aftermath of my life would have been if the same scenario had played out, but without her. To be left childless after the bad choices my partner made would have resulted in a very different Erica. I can imagine many versions of that Erica, but ultimately, I'll never know what she would have been like, and I don't want to. I'm grateful that I chose Irie's father and that we intentionally chose together to bring her earth-side. I'm grateful for the ways the demise of our relationship transpired, because it forced me to be a good mom—to rise to every occasion and push myself to figure out who I am and the things I need my daughter to know.

Motherhood is in large part about sacrifice and doing a lot of things you don't feel like doing. But so is life. The positives and negatives of my choices have led to my becoming the woman that I am today. And I am fucking proud of her. My story isn't any different from yours. In fact, maybe yours is harder, riddled with more pain, tragedy, or loss. However, I truly believe that Spirit, God, or whatever you believe in doesn't give you more than you can handle. The moment I started saying yes and following my divine intuition is the moment my life started. Irie was the catalyst to reinventing who I am and inspiring my purpose. Never in a million years would I have imagined that the girl who never wanted to have kids would have a platform dedicated to supporting and empowering mothers around the world. That's wild to me even now. I think deep down I always did know that I would be a good mom—that I had gifts and lessons to share and a legacy to leave behind in the form of a human and not just the fruits of my labor.

Fear, trauma, and the concern that I might have to do it alone were driving factors when I used to think that I would never have children. People have often asked me whether I might have more children now that I've conquered these fears. The answer is that I am open to all the possibilities, because that's how life gets fun. I've learned so many lessons by surrendering and replacing all my nos with yeses. Until I became a mother, I never realized what an honor it is to be one—to have this dignified opportunity to shape and influence what the world looks like for my child. I, and you, make the rules of how we define a good mom who makes bad choices. My choices don't define me, but they do lead me to making better ones and standing proudly in all of them.

You know the saying "Everything happens for a reason"? Well, it does—even the hard shit, even the shit that takes years to understand. The gift and curse of being a mother is the incessant reminder that you can't give up. You have to be there through your child's innocence and joy, tantrums, unsolicited hugs and love, and back talk; the gifts make every negative experience worth the effort. Simply put, Irie is my reason. She is my meditation: my ultimate practice of taking deep breaths and paying attention to what is happening in the present moment, looking on the brighter side and not taking life so seriously. She is my teacher, my mirror, my pain in the ass, my confidant, and my best friend—my good kid who made me a good mom.

A LETTER TO IRIE

Hi, Irie bear. I'm not sure when you'll read this. but wherever we are in our journey as mother and daughter, I want you to know one thing: I really tried my best. I know that there may have been moments in your life when I fell short, but I hope my shortcomings taught you valuable lessons about how you will resolve those moments as an individual and with your own kids, should you choose to have them.

Parents aren't perfect people. We fuck up sometimes. We miss the mark. I always try, however, to be a good example to you while also making myself proud. It took me a little while to find my flow, and you are the reason I did! You gave me purpose. I know that sounds corny, but it's true.

I hope I didn't make raising you look too easy, because it hasn't been. It's been hard work, dedication, mom guilt, sacrifice, fielding different opinions about what I should do. Being your primary parent during your younger years put a lot of pressure on me to be the best mom and person possible for you, but I wouldn't have had it any other way. Even though your father and I didn't play out how we thought we would, I need you to know that we brought you into this world in love. I love your father for the gift of you. His role in your existence is one I can never repay him for, because you, my love, are priceless.

Irie, you have been a teacher to me, and I hope that throughout our relationship I have made you feel that you have a voice in the decisions I've made for us. Your opinions matter to me, and your perspective is valuable, even when I don't agree. I wanted you to always know the honest truth so that you had choices—a variety of paths to choose from. I hope you know that you can literally do whatever the fuck you want. I mean that. People will try to tell you this statement is a lie. Run from those people. Your father and I are proof that living out your dreams is your destiny. You are never too much, my love. Make mistakes and bad choices so that you can learn the things that feel good to you, that make you feel alive.

You have the gift of being a woman. This is a privilege that gives you powers beyond what small-minded people will ever understand. You are the bearer of light and life; there is nothing you can't achieve. Take advantage of this gift, and tap into the powers of the divine feminine. Follow your intuition, because it's rarely wrong. Try to preserve your softness in a world that will do everything it can to make you hard.

Whenever you get scared, Mommy will be there as soon as I can. Even when I'm gone, I'm never really. Remember what I told you: energy never dies. Trust the gifts that you've chosen to adopt from our journeys together and those you've taken on your own. I want you to be your own person, not a version of me. You are enough as you are—more than enough.

Baby girl, I am so proud of you. From the moment you were born, I knew you'd shift the energy of the room and take control of your divine path. Don't be afraid to let go—to relinquish control and say yes to the things that seem a little scary. Even as a child, you were very grounded and reasonable. Those are beautiful qualities that make a mother sleep easy at night. But, baby, don't forget that in comfort also comes complacency. Settling will do nothing for your higher purpose and good. Please know that your own happiness is queen, even in love and motherhood.

I know that sometimes I had to be away from you, but I had to choose myself often so that I could show up as my full self for you. All my choices haven't been good, but I was learning, and I still am. Our relationship is the most important one I've ever had, and I hope that I've made you proud. I hope that you can love me through my imperfections and know that, even though I am not the perfect mom, I am the right mom for you. I am always by your side, forever and ever.

Te amo mucho,

Mama

MILAH

When I was choosing a name for my daughter, "Luna" spoke to me because my zodiac sign, Cancer, is often referred to as "moon child," and "luna" is Latin for "moon." Since birth, Luna has been living up to her name, shining brightly and leading me in my darkest hours. "Behati," her middle name, means "she who brings blessings," which seemed appropriate because she was born on Thanksgiving Day. Spirit was looking out, because Luna Behati has brought nothing but light and blessings since the day I met her.

Honestly, I was afraid of becoming a mother, not necessarily because I thought I would be terrible at it, but because I recognized that any wrong move could result in years of trauma and therapy. As I was growing up, my mom and I had a tumultuous relationship, and so a part of me had a lot of fear about having a daughter—fear that I would disappoint her, fear that she'd grow up and hate me. As a child, seeing my girlfriends have really close relationships with their moms irritated me. Watching my friends be affectionate with their mothers made me cringe; it felt "extra" and needy to me, but actually I was just envious. I've had to be extra careful not to take the style of parenting I received and automatically copy and paste it into my life. Like so much about parenting, that's easier said than done. When you're pregnant, you may have big plans about doing everything your parents didn't do and being extra perfect, but real-life parenting is much more difficult than hypothetical parenting.

I have been asked, "How do you think your daughter will

feel when she gets older and sees your explicit and personal stories all over the internet?" My response is and will always be the same: I'm raising a daughter who gets to watch me show up unapologetically as my real self, something I didn't get to witness my mother do. All I can do is lead by example; by living in my truth, I am inevitably showing Luna that her truth is always enough.

I believe there is nothing more important than teaching your children to live and walk in their truth. When our kids feel empowered in exactly who they are, they never have to seek validation from any outside source. Am I worried that Luna will grow up and be just like me? Not at all. I think I'm great, but that's not the point. I know I'm raising someone who knows the full me and also knows she does not have to be exactly like me. I respect her, her needs, her personal style, her choices. I have been particularly careful about keeping her free while also giving her the tools to tap into her intuition when situations and people don't align with her spirit. I'd like to believe that empowering our kids and giving them the gift of confidence is far more crucial than instilling fear. The world will do that anyway, especially when it comes to little girls.

I try my absolute hardest to go to great lengths not to project the ideas of the patriarchy on my blooming little lady. "Luna, what kind of mom do you think you will be?" I asked her once, looking in the rearview mirror at her in the back seat of the car.

"Not one at all. I don't want kids. I want to be an artist," said seven-year-old Luna.

"Amazing!"

Motherhood will always present us with opportunities to create more compassionate, knowledgeable, free-thinking humans. In a world full of assholes, raise a lover. Parenthood will always contain uncomfortable situations that we would like to avoid because our parents avoided them, but when uncomfortable circumstances arise, we can either run from them or take the opportunity to shift the story. I urge you to lean in. When the sex topic comes up, talk about it, honestly. When the masturbation conversation comes up, normalize it. Just because you may have learned certain topics were taboo doesn't mean they still are. Talk to your kids before they learn some bullshit from their peers.

I wish I could say that this journey morphed me into the perfect parent and that I have all the answers and all the tools, but I don't. I still have things to learn and unlearn about parenting. Nobody ever tells you how difficult it is to mother a small human while mothering yourself. We are forever learning and evolving on our life journeys; I still feel like a child myself in some ways. At every age, I discover new things about how humans develop. Truth is, we as mothers birth our children into this realm, but they are simply souls, like us—souls with different soul missions, learning different lessons, and seeking different things. We do not own our children; we have the gift of guiding them.

I'd be lying if I said that Luna hasn't been my teacher in more ways than one. I've had to become comfortable being the student some days. I know I have for sure been a teacher to my own mother, and that's the beauty in being open to giving and receiving in this role.

Motherhood is being both a teacher and a student all the time.

I am grateful that *Good Moms Bad Choices* has opened the path of self-exploration and healing for me. Taking the time to acknowledge and heal my own childhood trauma has made me a more intentional and much softer person and parent. Of course, I still struggle all the time. I am seven years in and still can't believe I have to do school drop-offs and pickups, pack lunches with personalized love letters, and go to all those Sunday soccer games. I am always pinching myself in disbelief. I am prouder than ever to have the opportunity to raise a woman unafraid of shaking shit up—a soldier in the world, if you will. Women are still struggling for their rightful place in the world, and I'm glad Luna will be prepared to sprinkle her razzle-dazzle all over this fight for the return of the divine feminine.

Life is about living to the fullest and sharing that joy with your children. When you live in joy, it's contagious. You in turn teach your children to prioritize themselves and prioritize their joy. I am confident that I am giving my child the tools of healing and the power to stand ten toes down in her truth at all times. I've given my child the opportunity to understand that her mother isn't perfect, but I'm honest and ever evolving. I hope that Luna gives herself the same grace, to grow, learn, heal, and evolve as she moves through this sometimes unforgiving world.

When I was pregnant, because I was expecting a girl, I thought about my relationship with my own mother a lot. I wondered whether the relationship I'd have with Luna would mimic the relationship I had with my own mom. I never felt I knew her, probably because she didn't know herself. That notion has always been a driving force behind my parenting style. I'm grateful my relationship with my mother made me ferociously seek my purpose, by any means necessary. That's the thing about motherhood: it comes with no rule book.

I hope you take from this book one thing above all: forgiveness and deep compassion for yourself. The compassion I withheld from my mother is now the compassion I offer myself. We all deserve forgiveness and room for healing. Healing is the road to growth, and growth is the way you discover your people and your purpose. My hope is that Luna understands that her peace and happiness are always worth fighting for and that her power is infinite, that her intuition is worth listening to, and that her truth is always more valuable than a lie.

A LETTER TO LUNA

Luna B, by far the most incredible experience of my life has been raising you and watching you grow. You are my life's work and my best accomplishment. You are sweet, so funny, wise beyond your years, compassionate, and wildly creative—a masterpiece. I need you to know that you are my reason. When you made me a mommy, I discovered myself and my purpose. The moment I met you, something shifted. You were the spark that brought me to the life I dreamed of, and I hope that the work you have witnessed me create inspires you to do whatever the fuck you want to do.

You make the rules, and you can break the rules, too. You are truly my bestie, and I look forward to more sushi dates, dance parties, cuddles, and world travels together. My main hope is that I can give you the power you have given me. You come from a badass, trailblazing mama who has never taken no for an answer, and I know you are a force to be reckoned with—a positive force of change.

I know I have made sacrifices at your expense. I've spent hours and hours with you without being present in order to make my dreams come true and to create the life of our dreams. I hope that one day you understand the importance of the work I am doing and that you can forgive me for those days when it interfered with our time together. Building a business is much like raising a baby. I hope that you are proud and inspired by my journey. I want to thank you for pushing me and being patient with me. Please understand that I am not perfect; I've made many mistakes. I am still learning and will continue to learn, apologize, and strive to be the best version of myself for you. No matter what, I am always here for you, to pick you up when you fall down. No matter how big or grown you get, I will always have your back and your front.

Stay shining, keep taking up space, stay firm in who you are, and always, always, trust your good choices and learn from your bad ones. I hope that when and if you dive deep into the

Good Moms Bad Choices catalog (when you're old enough), you can laugh, cry, learn from my life experiences, and understand me even better because I've been learning, too.

Love you always and forever,
in this lifetime and every lifetime,

Mama

Conclusion

Mama, you made it! At least to the end of this book. This is the part where you take the pieces that feel good to you and apply them to your own life. Our motherhood is not your motherhood; our journey is not your journey. The lessons we've learned may not be the lessons you need to learn, but the one thing we'd like to leave you with is the knowledge that you are a good mom—as a matter of fact, you're a fucking great mom!

You know all those unwritten rules that society and the patriarchy have created to regulate what women's freedoms, lives, and choices look like? Well, they're fake. You make the rules because you are the alchemist of your own life. The dualities of our existence are intended to inspire you to take chances. Explore everything! Say yes more! Stop waiting for someone or something else to show up. You are the person you've been waiting for. Release your expectations, and happily invite in the unexpected.

If you feel alone in motherhood, congratulations—you have found your tribe! The *Good Moms Bad Choices* community is a judgment-free zone where women and mothers are linking up, talking their shit, and sharing their real stories. You don't even have to stalk a random girl at a bar and make her your friend. Now go be the good mom and the bad bitch we know you are!

Xoxo,

The Good Moms

Acknowledgments

MILAH

Wow, getting to this point has been perhaps the scariest and most exhilarating journey I have ever been on. I would like to thank my platonic wife and best friend, Erica, for taking the front seat and joining me on this wild ride—all gas, no breaks. You have given me the gift of staying grounded and a confidence in myself I hadn't discovered before the birth of *Good Moms Bad Choices*. Thank you for loving me as I am, and for never once telling me I am too much or too little. Thank you for trusting in this process with me and for answering this call on the road less traveled; our entity is just getting started.

Becoming an author has been my dream since I was a little girl, partially because of my father, Myles, who gave me the gift of gab. Thank you for never censoring Howard Stern on those morning rides to elementary school. I learned the gift of being my unapologetic true self from you, a trait I now understand is priceless. Thank you to my mother, Joann, who has shown me through her actions how to be resilient and take no shit from anyone. You have always pushed me to be the best version of myself and to live to my fullest potential. I want to thank my brother, Mazi, for being my first baby and for loving me unconditionally. To my feisty Grandmother Shockley, I get my strength from you. You have taught me to never settle, and shown me how to truly live, as long as I'm living. Thank you to my first high school bestie, Ashley Bradley, for introducing me to the world of literature I could relate to and for encouraging me to write. Thank you to my first adult bestie, Danielle, for supporting me in this motherhood journey like no other and always encouraging me to take my writing more seriously. To Nisha and Brandon Espy, for bringing Erica and Irie into my life and for always supporting us and believing in our vision. Ca$hley, thank you for pushing and inspiring me every step of the way, and being the prototype of how hard work really pays off. To my cousin Chris, who has always shown up for me and shown me the many paths to spirit and manifesting, I am forever grateful for your open mind and our candid conversations. To Shani, for being one of my most magical guides and friends. Thank you for your honesty over the years and for sharing your most precious gifts—Isa, Rhia, and Asandra—with me and for being the dopest example of a single mom living to the beat of her own drum I have ever witnessed. Thank you to my other best friend Mirah, for some of the best "bad choices" of my life; you are a fuckin rider! Thank you to my entire tribe, for the endless love and support. I am at peace knowing I found my people. To my lover, Orlando, thank you for pouring into me and loving me and Lu in ways I could have never imagined; you are truly a unicorn, and I am grateful for our unwavering friendship. To my daughter, Luna, thank you for being my reason and my very best friend. Thank you for your wisdom and honesty at the tender age of seven. Finally, thank you to every woman I have met along the way and those I haven't who have tuned in, written in, and given us the support we needed to live in our truth. I feel your energy daily.

ERICA

Many people have pushed and nurtured me on my journey to writing this book and becoming a good mom who makes bold choices. First, I'd like to thank Jamilah, because without her none of this would be possible. Her authenticity has taught me to stand ten toes in mine even when I want to retreat. To my mother, my voice of reason and my example that there is no ceiling. I love you, I love you. To my Tawney, the spice in my bloodline who loves her grandchildren with all her might. My papa, Howard, who always saw the silver lining and started recording my voice at age six on our weekly rides to who-knows-where. My father, who always supports me no matter what. I forgive you, and I wouldn't change a thing. To Flor, *Irie y yo te queremos mucho. Eres un regalo de dios.* To my brother and Rory, two peas in a pod who always save the day. I love you. To Sebastian, my rock and sounding board. I love you so much it fucking hurts crabby new. To Romo, a.k.a. Tia, my forever Scorpio sister. Dana and Davida, the mophead crew, and my first girl tribe. My Jared, "koi," I love you so. To Nisha: without you there would be no *Good Moms*. Thank you for always seeing the vision. I love you. To Ashley, who never lets me stop raising the bar, and to our Tribe grouptext who puts up with all our shit. Thank you for all your honest input and support. To all the women who have been teachers along the way and who have empowered and shown me that it is more than okay to take up space—that I was put here to do that. To the men who show up for me and restored my faith and trust. Thank you. To my ancestors who sacrificed so much so that I could have the privilege of walking this life the way I do. There are no words to express my gratitude. I promise to take every chance you couldn't, and celebrate for us every chance I get. And to Irie, thank you for holding me accountable, even at seven years old. You are my forever bestie and my reason. Thank you for choosing me. I love you.

Collectively we would like to thank our agents, Tess, Clare, and Mark, for believing in us and guiding us through the process of writing this book. Thank you to our *GMBC* team past and present. Without you we'd still be sitting in a dining room filming episodes on one microphone. Thank you to all the guests of the show whose voices helped evolve us as women and push forward so many necessary conversations. Thank you to our Good Moms Tribe all over the world. Your messages and support helped two lonely single moms find their voice and purpose.

Finally, thank you, the reader, for sharing your time and energy as you flipped through the pages of our stories. We're best friends now. Welcome to the Tribe.